THE PRO KNOW-HOW™ BOOK OF

Logo Theory

How Branding Design Really Works

A. Michael Shumate

PRO KNOW HOW BOOKS™

Pro Know-How™ Books are not written for dummies or for complete idiots. Instead, they are written by experienced professionals for people who have aspirations to acquire skills at a professional level through study and applied effort.

Table of Contents

Introduction

The first day of teaching new college students, I tell them to call me Michael, not Professor Shumate or Mr. Shumate. Then I tell them that if they forget my name, they can always call me Grand Poobah. The term comes from the Gilbert and Sullivan musical *The Mikado* and is one of many titles that an officious character has bestowed upon himself. It has come to mean "anyone with no real authority but who acts otherwise" (as defined, appropriately enough, in Wikipedia). There you have it. I will speak with great authority where I have none, except that which experience has given me.

What is my experience? I graduated with a BFA degree in Graphic Design, and I've been a professional designer and illustrator for nearly fifty years. My design and illustration work has been used by the National Football League, Simon & Schuster, Kelly Services, *British Airways Magazine*, the Screen Actors Guild, *Business Week* and Prudential, to name a few. In addition to freelancing, I was a professor of Graphic Design and Illustration at St. Lawrence College in Ontario, where I taught for twenty-five years.

In my professional design career, I have created dozens of corporate-identity designs, but in my teaching career I have guided students to create thousands of identity designs. It is that kind of perspective I wish to share.

I won't quote other books or authorities to justify my position; I'll just visually show each principle or issue and let your own eyes bear witness to you what is true. It is part of human nature that we can see a fault in another more quickly than in ourselves.

As a teacher I had an obligation to evaluate the work of my students and give concrete reasons for the grades awarded. I found that it was not good enough to point out failings; I had to try to teach how to avoid those failings in the first place. That exercise, over 25 years, has given me insights into the principles of branding design that I have not seen shared anywhere else. I wish to pass them on to you.

This will be a personal book, from me to you, a fellow designer. My hope is to save you a few years of trial and error and speed you on to succeed in your corporate-identity design.

Maybe you will look at this art of branding design with new eyes and perhaps be a little wiser and more directed in your work.

I hope so. I wish you success.

A. Michael Shumate
BFA, RGD Emeritus
Professor Emeritus
of St. Lawrence College
a.k.a. Grand Poobah

Chapter One

Foundational Principles of Graphic Design

Professional, Prima Donna or Artsy-Fartsy?

Prima donna was originally a term for the principal woman soloist in an opera production, literally the "first lady." The term is also used to describe a self-important person who may be capable artistically, but is also insufferably demanding and difficult to please. Now we use it mostly as an insult. It implies a person who is rude, proud, self-centered and opportunistic—a talented brat.

While we can see that artistic achievers are sometimes afflicted with these negative human traits, we ought not swallow the lie that their creative achievement came *because* of those traits. It came in spite of them.

In contrast, a professional has both pride and humility. Here is a simple definition of a professional: a person who can do a good job and who works in good faith for the benefit of his or her client. A professional puts the client above self. He or she takes appropriate pride in putting the job first and in being capable of consistent excellence. The humility is recognition that the performer is not the center of attraction. The performance is.

If I go to see my dentist and he says, "How about a root canal today? You don't really need one, but I love to do them," I would consider him to be terribly unprofessional. I would never return and would do what I could to see that he doesn't ever practice dentistry again.

If I consulted a lawyer about a simple matter, and he suggested that we launch a law suit, when much more direct or less costly methods had not been explored, I might feel the same.

Any professional I hire is supposed to act in *my* best interests.

Designers, being in an artistic occupation, often have to prove they are not artsy-fartsy flakes, but rather, can be a valued part of a whole business team. We can and should be key players that bring specialized expertise and prove that good design benefits a business.

And so it is in corporate-identity design: a professional branding designer is one who creates identities in the best interest of the client, not one who does what feels most "creative" or what might get recognition from peers. A professionally designed identity is one that will work well for the client in all situations, not in just some formats.

As this book unfolds, I hope I will be able to explain each design principle clearly enough that we can agree, in the end, that there are solid principles of identity design that we can adopt to become, in every sense of the word, professional designers.

Bedrock Principles

In my first month of teaching college Branding Design, I reviewed a student's concept for a logo project. I told him that his approach wouldn't work.

He asked why.

I told him I didn't know why. It just wouldn't. At that moment I remembered my father once saying, "Because I said so." I hadn't liked it then, and I knew that my answer to the student was equally arbitrary, unhelpful and even ridiculous. Still, I knew in my gut that his work was violating some underlying and important principle. But I couldn't articulate what that principle was. That day, I made a solemn commitment to learn the whys, not just the whats, of graphic design.

I never gave up on that commitment. Over the years, while supervising thousands of student projects (as well as creating my own professional work and considering the work of others), I studied, pondered and probed. I watched various fads and fashions in branding design come and go. On the other hand, I observed that identities by great designers like Saul Bass, Paul Rand and Chermayeff & Giesmar were used for decades—some for more than half a century—and still looked modern and fresh.

Bedrock principles in graphic design trump fad and fashion every time. You can break those rules, but, in reality, only your work breaks, like waves against the rocks. There are few areas where this is more evident than in designing corporate identity. Designers whose identities violate those principles will find that, sooner or later, their creations will be replaced.

The underlying principles of identity design don't change. Those who cater to temporary swings in taste will find their work goes out of style quickly. Designers who think that they can do anything and call it an identity don't understand the nature of identities. Those who vainly seek to be on the leading edge find out, more often than not, that they are on the bleeding edge. Those who refuse to learn the craft of identity design are forever mere amateurs.

What is the Purpose of Graphic Design?

I was once in an elevator with the custodian of our building. I knew him by name, and he knew I was a professor of graphic design. This day he proudly announced to me that he planned to open his own graphic design business.

"Really?" I responded with genuine curiosity. This man had never mentioned graphic design before.

"Yes. I just got a new computer and now *I can choose fonts*."

I was dumfounded. It was apparent that he thought that choosing fonts was all there was to graphic design. To reinforce his position, he continued, "I designed my first brochure last night, and I used twenty-eight different fonts!"

Mercifully, the elevator door opened on my floor and I got out.

This kind of idea is all too common, even among graphic design students and a few lesser practitioners. They feel a graphic designer's job is to "jazz-up" the content or "make it look cool" or "make it fancy."

While jazzing-up a design may be appropriate in some circumstances, it might be disastrous in others, and it is not the underlying purpose of good graphic design.

So, what is the purpose of graphic design?

To aid communication.

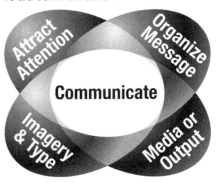

This can be accomplished in several ways:

ATTRACTING ATTENTION. In our world of never-ending messages, one must first get a pair of eyes to look at a message before it can be communicated. Designers use tools like typography, layout, color and imagery to do this. So esthetics do matter.

ORGANIZING THE MESSAGE. Complex messages or bodies of information must be broken down into manageable and logical subsets as well as a logical order. This is essential in media such as brochures and web sites.

USING IMAGERY & TYPE CORRECTLY. A given design can lead with imagery or with type. Type can be a kind of imagery in itself. When used together, there needs to be a hierarchy in the elements to control the viewer's eyes and the communication experience.

USING THE CORRECT MEDIA or OUTPUT This may seem too obvious to mention, but the physical form of the media can provide advantages as well as limitations. A poster does not work like a website. A brochure has different parameters from a business card. Signage is not the same as a magazine ad.

All of these considerations can distract us from a basic principle: the primary job of graphic design is to facilitate communication. Anything that compromises that core function is counter-productive.

Form Follows....?

Recently I shopped for a tool to help me get rid of dandelions on my lawn. I have an aversion to herbicides, and snipping the tops of the plants does little. The roots, which are several inches deep, must come out. I came home with a dandelion digger that looked both sturdy and elegant, ostensibly a good design. But when I went to use it, I found the job harder than I had expected, and it left gaping two-inch holes in my lawn.

The next day, I exchanged the tool for one that wasn't as expensive or attractive, but was easier to use and left much smaller holes—more like ones you get when you aerate your lawn. Since the primary function of the tool was not appearance or fashion, I was fine with the way it looked. Its function was paramount.

One of the most ubiquitous catchphrases in art and craft is "Form Follows Function." And it contains a lot of truth.

If a form impedes function or creates new problems, it is a poor design. While it is not wrong to re-evaluate the specific function we might be seeking, the form we choose had better not impede that core function.

It is sometimes easy to get distracted from the essential function of a creative project. This is especially true when esthetics is part of the function. But esthetics is not the only function of a corporate identity. Clear thinking must override gut impulses in this area.

What is the function of a corporate identity?

1. To be seen and recognized instantly,

2. To appropriately and positively represent the business/organization/product being identified,

3. To be consistently reproducible across all media,

4. To be flexible enough to accommodate various design and media requirements.

If we create a design that fails in any of these four functions, we have failed to create a workable design. Period.

Some people know how to make solid, useful identities. For many others, the process is hit-or-miss. Some seem fixated on doing something that has

9

never been done before, not only in their specific design, but in their very approach. Perhaps they believe that because they produced something new, they have been terribly creative. What they may forget to do is test their finished design against the four functions above. If it doesn't pass *all* four of those tests, such a creation shouldn't have been born in the first place.

That may have been why people didn't do it that way before. That way doesn't work.

In the end, creativity is the ability to find the best way to solve a problem. Period.

Creativity is often characterized as a new way of doing something. That is because a new problem sometimes requires an new solution. That's why we notice it. But the core of creativity is not that it is new. That's a common fallacy of logic called Association with Causation—a false notion that because two events occur together, one causes the other. Corn and pumpkins often ripen at the same time, but the corn does not make the pumpkins ripen, or vice versa.

For any problem, there may be many new and different approaches that will NOT provide a solution. Theoretically only a few, or perhaps even only one, will succeed.

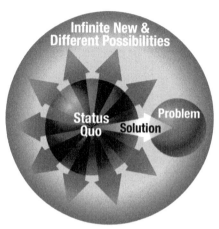

A problem does not always reside outside of the status quo. It may touch that circle tangentially. This means that the most suitable solution will not require anything new to solve it. This is a common irritant to those who desperately aspire to their notion of "creativity" at all costs. They insist that newness is an essential part of any solution. This fixation is almost epidemic in creative fields like graphic design. The tragic flaw is that the new and unusual approach may fail to solve the problem at hand. Sad to say, many design annuals abound in examples of "bleeding edge" design—the cutting edge that has gone too far and doesn't work. The form does not follow the function.

And if a design doesn't function in the client's best interests, it isn't professional (even if the designer gets paid for it). Sooner or later the client will go elsewhere.

Designing identities that work in all situations is eminently doable—if you know the principles of good design, which we're about to get to.

Basic Principles of Design

We live in a graphic savvy culture. Design infuses everything from the gadgets we use to communicate and play, to the clothes we wear, to the bottle our shampoo comes in. Every brochure we pick up, every ad in a magazine, every commercial on TV is designed. It is said that the average person now is exposed to more than 3,000 images a day.

But just because we eat every day doesn't mean we know how to cook.

Just because we **EAT** every day doesn't mean we know how to **COOK**

It is estimated that more than 35,000,000 copies of the Adobe Creative Suite (Photoshop, Illustrator, InDesign, etc.) or other graphics-capable software are in use today. Many users have no design training. As a result, bad design abounds. Even those with formal training don't necessarily know what they're doing. Many schools now focus training more on software and less on design principles. People who know only the programs, not design, are sometimes hired to teach new generations of graphic designers. Result? Graphic design graduates with a lack of good grounding in their field.

In opposition to the tide of design illiteracy, let's agree on four basic principles.

11

Principle #1:
Simplicity is the Soul of Good Design

Beginning designers often get to a stage in a project where they ask themselves, "What else does this need?"

More often they should be asking, "What do I need to delete?" This is especially true with corporate-identity design. The best of these are spare and are the more memorable and effective for it.

Simplicity is the SOUL of good Design

Principle #2:
Computers Don't Design for You

Even if we could plug computers directly into our brains, we would have to know what something *should* look like before we could design it.

I would never design identities without a vector computer program. These programs offer capabilities that cannot be duplicated by hand. Regardless, computers don't design, and computers don't draw, in the esthetic sense. It is a sad reality that computers don't do what we *want* them to do. They do what we *tell* them to do. It's up to us to know which shapes, sizes, relationships and colors will work. I call this Visual Knowledge. If we don't have Visual Knowledge, the computer won't supply it. Computers supply mathematically based processes, not knowledge.

A computer won't tell you if your shapes are esthetically mismatched. A computer can tell you what size your elements are, but it doesn't know if those sizes are appropriate together. That's your job.

In the end, if you can't draw, you can't draw on the computer. If you can't design, you can't design on the computer.

Early in my teaching career, I taught a course called Graphic Techniques. It covered many difficult esthetic and manual skills that graphic designers used to need. One of my students was on the brink of failing. He begged me to let him have the benefit of the doubt. "I'm a whiz on the computer," he said. "You'll see." He barely passed that course, and when he got to the computer-based design, his work was horrible. His designs were all techno-crap. The lesson: computers don't supply esthetics.

Principle #3: Beware BYC Design

When I began graphic design, we didn't use computers. If we wanted a gradient in a design, there were two ways to get it.

1. We hired an airbrush artist to paint the gradient, then had it photographed, photo-separated and spliced into plate negatives by a photoengraver.

2. We could have the photoengravers (if they knew how) make the gradients directly. Either way, some of the control was relinquished to the airbrush artists and photoengravers.

In both cases gradients were so expensive, they were seldom worth squandering the design budget on. Nowadays there are very few airbrush artists (good thing, too; with all the heavy-metal pigments in the air, this was a hazardous profession). Most airbrushing is done in Photoshop now. Also, the whole profession of photoengraving has almost vanished. Our designs go from the computer directly to plates without anyone having to make color separations (which used to be expensive in its own right) or stripping together and registering the separate negatives from which to burn the printing plates.

Some of the processes that used to be so expensive are easy to do now; the only thing they cost today's designers is the trouble of clicking a certain button. That has created an epidemic of BYC Design. What does it mean? "Because You Can." That is an extremely shallow reason for doing something. Sadly, when it's the designer's only reason, the design usually suffers.

Principle #4: Beware JTBD Design

Only slightly better is JTBD Design, "Just to Be Different."

Not that novelty is a bad thing. It's great if it doesn't cause other problems like bad legibility, poor reproduction, or greater costs for the client (remember, not acting in the client's best interest is inherently unprofessional). Measured against the possible downsides, novelty alone can be a poor bargain.

Beware of "Just to Be Different" Design. (Given the moral of this story, this kitschy type treatment is ironically appropriate.)

Hang on.

We'll get to some design principles you can really buy into.

Legibility and Contrast

Basic Terms

Before we launch into a discussion of color and contrast, let's make sure we are using the same language. Three terms may be used in describing any given color.

First is hue. Hue is how colors distinguish themselves from each other in the rainbow or spectrum. It is also how colors are differentiated around a color wheel.

Second is saturation, the relative richness or dullness of a color. All colors in the spectrum are fully saturated (except at the ends, where they lapse into black). Dusty rose is less saturated (or more neutral) than pink. Olive is a less saturated version of yellow-green.

The third term is value. That's just the inherent lightness or darkness of a color. Going around a properly constructed color wheel, the lightest color is yellow and the darkest is blue.

Of the more than two million colors that a normal human eye can discern, each one can be described using these three terms, the way we could use three axis points to determine the position of something in three-dimensional space.

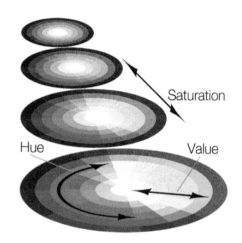

Saturation

Hue   Value

Legibility

When we can see and read what is written or perceive the elements of a picture, we call that legibility. Legibility is a function of contrast.

Legibility is a function of contrast
Legibility is a function of contrast
Legibility is a function of contrast
Legibility is a function of contrast
Legibility is a function of contrast
Legibility is a function of contrast
Legibility is a function of contrast
Legibility is a function of contrast
Legibility is a function of contrast

Of the three qualities of color we just defined—hue, saturation and value—the one that matters most for contrast is value. Saturation and hue hardly make a difference, especially when distance or small size is involved.

To sum up so far: legibility is a function of contrast, and contrast is a function of value.

Nothing compensates for a lack of legibility. No concept. No style or fashion. No coolness factor. I repeat: Nothing compensates for a lack of legibility. Without it, no one even sees

or correctly perceives your work. It's fundamental.

A good tool for accurately describing values is tint percentage, developed in the printing industry. Halftone tints cover an area with small uniform grid of dots on a paper, often smaller than can be seen with the naked eye. In a 70% halftone tint, 70% of the paper area is covered in ink and only 30% of the paper has no ink. These halftone tint percentages should be second nature to graphic designers.

Surprint 10%	20%	30%	40%	50%
	20%	30%	40%	50%
	90%	80%	70%	60%
100% Reverse	90%	80%	70%	60%

Halftone tint percentages are a convenient way to describe value in concrete terms.

Contrast Differential

The amount of contrast between type and a background can be calculated by subtracting the lesser value percentage from the greater. A good rule of thumb for excellent contrast is 60% difference or more. Black type on white paper is a 100% difference, the greatest contrast possible, whereas 35% contrast differential is minimal.

Is it physically possible to read below that threshold? Yes, of course. But is it convenient or comfortable? No. And what is the function of graphic design? To aid communication, not impede it. Why would any sane designer try to make the printed message anything less than convenient or comfortable to read?

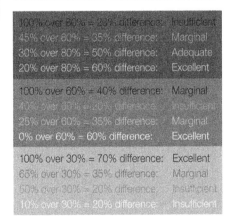

100% over 80% = 20% difference: Insufficient
45% over 80% = 35% difference: Marginal
30% over 80% = 50% difference: Adequate
20% over 80% = 60% difference: Excellent

100% over 60% = 40% difference: Marginal
40% over 60% = 20% difference: Insufficient
25% over 60% = 35% difference: Marginal
0% over 60% = 60% difference: Excellent

100% over 30% = 70% difference: Excellent
65% over 30% = 35% difference: Marginal
50% over 30% = 20% difference: Insufficient
10% over 30% = 20% difference: Insufficient

Where Intuition Fails

If one accepts the logic of the foregoing, one would naturally think that a designer would be safe to place black type on a background as dark as 40% or 50%. The reality is that such type is tiresome, even oppressive, to read.

Why is that?

Because white reflects all available light and black absorbs it. Therefore, white is a stimulus to our visual system, and black is the absence of a stimulus. So when we read black type on a 50% background we are seeing a non-stimulus against a half-stimulus.

On the other hand, when we read white type on the same background, we are seeing a strong stimulus against a half stimulus. That's why it's inherently easier and why reversed type at the minimal cutoff seems to have better contrast. Even so, the 35% minimum contrast is a useful rule of thumb.

Black reflects no light, an abscence of stimulus
Black reflects no light, an abscence of stimulus
Black reflects no light, an abscence of stimulus
White relects light, and is a very strong stimulus
White relects light, and is a very strong stimulus
White relects light, and is a very strong stimulus

It is naturally easier to read white type over a 50% gray background than it is to read black type.

In practical application, the cutoff for comfortable surprinting versus reversing

isn't at the 50% mark, but at about 35%. Does that strike you as odd?

Maybe, until you remember the Golden section, the Fibonacci sequence, and its modern counterpart, the rule of thirds.

0%	10%	20%	30%	40%	50%	60%	70%	80%	90%	100%
			White	White	White	White	White	White	White	White
			White	White	White	White	White	White	White	White
		10%	10%	10%	10%	10%	10%	10%	10%	10%
		10%	10%	10%	10%	10%	10%	10%	10%	10%
		20%	20%	20%	20%	20%	20%	20%	20%	20%
		20%	20%	20%	20%	20%	20%	20%	20%	20%
30%	30%	30%		30%	30%	30%	30%	30%	30%	30%
30%	30%	30%		30%	30%	30%	30%	30%	30%	30%
40%	40%	40%	40%		40%	40%	40%	40%	40%	40%
40%	40%	40%	40%		40%	40%	40%	40%	40%	40%
50%	50%	50%	50%	50%		50%	50%	50%	50%	50%
50%	50%	50%	50%	50%		50%	50%	50%	50%	50%
60%	60%	60%	60%	60%	60%		60%	60%	60%	60%
60%	60%	60%	60%	60%	60%		60%	60%	60%	60%
70%	70%	70%	70%	70%	70%	70%		70%	70%	70%
70%	70%	70%	70%	70%	70%	70%		70%	70%	70%
80%	80%	80%	80%	80%	80%	80%	80%		80%	80%
80%	80%	80%	80%	80%	80%	80%	80%		80%	80%
90%	90%	90%	90%	90%	90%	90%	90%	90%		90%
90%	90%	90%	90%	90%	90%	90%	90%	90%		90%
Black	Black	Black	Black	Black	Black	Black	Black	Black	Black	
Black	Black	Black	Black	Black	Black	Black	Black	Black	Black	

Logically, we would expect the cutoff between reversing and surprinting to be at the 50% line (red line). But in practice, reading dark surprinted type over 40% and 50% backgrounds is tiresome, even oppressive. Instead, the practical cutoff for reversing and surprinting is at the 35% mark (cyan line).

16

The ancient Greeks discovered a particular proportion that kept cropping up in many different places in nature. They called this the Golden Mean or the Golden Section. They considered it a divine ratio and sought to use it in some of their buildings and sculpture. Leonardo Fibonacci was a pre-Renaissance mathematician who discovered a sequence of numbers where each adjacent pair of numbers gave the Golden Section proportion more or less. In modern times, photographers and other students of visual arts are often instructed in the "law of thirds," which is that compositions will seem most dynamically balanced if major elements are placed within the picture plane at a location of 1/3 or 2/3.

Now that we've covered the basics of contrast in black and white, we'll cover its application to color next.

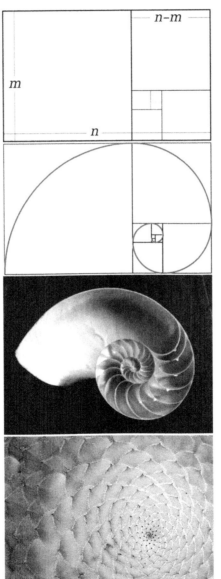

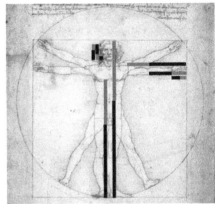

The Greeks found a proportion in geometry that is also found in nature, that they called the Golden Mean. The human body is replete with examples of the golden section.

Color and Contrast

Every Color has a Value

Though we may not have thought about it before, every color has a value. By definition, only white can be 0% and only black can be 100%. Just choosing colors for type that are very different in hue is no guarantee of legibility. It still comes down to value. A designer needs to ignore hue and saturation when selecting colors for type over colored backgrounds. The designer needs to learn to see the inherent value of each color to ensure there is sufficient contrast.

Special note: If excellent contrast is 60% contrast differential or greater, it is impossible to achieve excellent contrast over a 50% background.

Black type is a 100% value Blue type can be a 80% value Brown type can be a 70% value Gold type can be a 30% value Yellow type can be a 10% value White type is a 0% value	**Black type is a 100% value** Blue type can be a 80% value Gold type can be a 30% value Yellow type can be a 10% value White type is a 0% value
Black type is a 100% value Blue type can be a 80% value Brown type can be a 70% value Red type can be a 60% value Yellow type can be a 10% value White type is a 0% value	**Black type is a 100% value** Blue type can be a 80% value Brown type can be a 70% value Red type can be a 60% value Yellow type can be a 10% value White type is a 0% value
Black type is a 100% value Red type can be a 60% value Brown type can be a 70% value Gold type can be a 30% value Yellow type can be a 10% value White type is a 0% value	**Black type is a 100% value** Red type can be a 60% value Brown type can be a 70% value Gold type can be a 30% value Yellow type can be a 10% value White type is a 0% value
Black type is a 100% value Blue type can be a 80% value Red type can be a 60% value Gold type can be a 30% value Yellow type can be a 10% value White type is a 0% value	**Black type is a 100% value** Red type can be a 60% value Gold type can be a 30% value Yellow type can be a 10% value White type is a 0% value

Designers must always think of colors as values to assure enough contrast differential.

In the book covers here, we can see that the red type on a blue background is difficult to read in the title and nearly impossible to read in the smaller type. All you have to do is browse any online bookseller to see how often book cover designers make this mistake, and not just the self-published ones, either. This is so important because in our digital age, the first time millions of people will see any book cover, it is at 150 pixels high.

The Dreaded V Words

If the background and the type are close in hue and in value, the type will vanish. Here magenta type is on a red background.

If the background and type are very different in hue and close in value, then vibrating will occur. While this is more legible than vanishing, it makes up for it by being irritating and should be avoided at all costs. As with other issues created by values, these are exacerbated by small sizes or being viewed at a distance, such as in signage.

Close values create Vanishing and Vibrating. Both are disastrous to legibility

Difference in hue has very little bearing on contrast; only value provides it. And the damage is worse the smaller the type is or if it is lighter in weight. If you think this isn't a big deal, just try to view these covers from even a few feet away.

Busy Backgrounds

Type frequently needs to be placed over a photo or other imagery. If the background for type is busy, the type may be impossible to read. Busy backgrounds are defined as those in which both light and dark elements exist. No color of type will be easy to read over a busy background. Remember, the question is not, "Can the viewer eventually puzzle out what is written?" but rather, "Is this design helping or hurting communication?"

This doesn't mean that a background must always be a flat color. Just make sure that the values are either all light or all dark; then surprinted or reversed type will have a chance. However, if parts of the texture are in the mid-value range, it may be impossible to achieve excellent contrast (60% difference or more).

However, if all parts of a background, are either all dark or all light, a good contrast for type can be achieved

However, if all parts of a background, are either all dark or all light, a good contrast for type can be achieved

Question: What if the photo doesn't have either all dark texture or all light?

Answer: Time for an assist from Photoshop. :)

What color type can be easily read over a busy background?
What color type can be easily read over a busy background?
What color type can be easily read over a busy background?
What color type can be easily read over a busy background?
What color type can be easily read over a busy background?

What color type can be easily read over a busy background?
What color type can be easily read over a busy background?
What color type can be easily read over a busy background?
What color type can be easily read over a busy background?
What color type can be easily read over a busy background?

What color type can be easily read over a busy background?
What color type can be easily read over a busy background?
What color type can be easily read over a busy background?
What color type can be easily read over a busy background?
What color type can be easily read over a busy background?

The text says, "What color type can easily be read over a very busy background?" The answer: nothing will work. Don't put text over a busy background. Ever.

Widely Varying Backgrounds

A similar problem occurs over widely varying backgrounds, such as in a gradient that has light, mid and dark portions in its progression. Again the answer is: nothing will work well. Some parts will survive, maybe even have quite good contrast, but others will be illegible or at least compromised. Don't do it.

Does that mean that all gradients are useless?

No. But if text is to go over it, then limit the background gradient to half the value continuum (or less) and make the type the other value extreme. For instance, make the background mid to dark with light type over. Or else make

the background light to mid with dark type over (but remember that even black type isn't comfortably read on backgrounds darker than 35%).

What color is easily read over widely varying backgrounds?
What color is easily read over widely varying backgrounds?
What color is easily read over widely varying backgrounds?
What color is easily read over widely varying backgrounds?
What color is easily read over widely varying backgrounds?

What color is easily read over widely varying backgrounds?
What color is easily read over widely varying backgrounds?
What color is easily read over widely varying backgrounds?
What color is easily read over widely varying backgrounds?
What color is easily read over widely varying backgrounds?

What color is easily read over widely varying backgrounds?
What color is easily read over widely varying backgrounds?
What color is easily read over widely varying backgrounds?
What color is easily read over widely varying backgrounds?
What color is easily read over widely varying backgrounds?

A widely varying background is one where both light and dark values are found. No single color of type can give consistently good contrast over such a background. Some part is sure to have poor contrast.

When "Close Enough" isn't Close Enough

In baseball, you get three strikes before you're out. But in graphic design, there are times when two strikes are all you get. Sometimes only one. Consider outside signage, for instance. It will be viewed in variable lighting conditions. It may have to fight to be seen amid all sorts of visual distraction. The viewer may be moving fast and have only a split second to absorb the message. I would call outside signage a one-strike situation. What are other factors that reduce the amount of leeway a designer has? A challenging type font or an unfamiliar or difficult word up the ante.

Corporate identity is one area where you can strike out with one bad decision, especially when it involves poor contrast.

Anybody who has ever printed from a computer knows that what you see on the screen is often different from what appears on the printed page. Colors can appear too dark, too light, too warm, too cool, too washed-out, compared with their appearance on the computer monitor. Too often beginners think that the contrast in their design, as viewed on the computer monitor, is "close enough."

That is courting design disaster. One should always consider that the printing (or the viewer's monitor) will eat up some of your "good enough" margin.

A wise designer will always aim for excellent contrast, which is a contrast differential of 60% or more. The bare minimum is 35%. Don't consider fudging on those parameters.

These are the kinds of principles that will have a bearing on corporate-identity design.

The Doctrine of Coincide or Contrast

Here is a principle with many applications in graphic design: elements should either coincide or contrast. It is surprising how often this golden rule of design will answer a wide range of questions—choice of typography, layout, image style and color. We will look only at typography and layout here.

Getting two different sans serif fonts to work together is very difficult.
They don't coincide and they are too close to contrast.

(above) Helvetica Neue LT Std. Light and Gill Sans Light (same point size).

(at right) Georgia and Berhard Modern Std (same point size)

Font Choices

One of the easiest applications of Coincide or Contrast is in typography. It is very difficult to use two different sans-serif fonts together. There is not enough difference to provide meaningful contrast but too much difference to coincide.

Perhaps an example in a totally diifernt realm might illustrate. It's like wearing stripes and plaid together; it just doesn't work. Stripes with a plain fabric would give a nice contrast without visual violence. Plaid with a plain fabric could also work.

The same is true when using serif fonts: two different serif fonts are unlikely to work well together. They have too much difference to coincide, but not enough to contrast. They look mismatched because they are. They clash.

Getting two different serif fonts to work together is very difficult.
They don't coincide and they are too close to contrast.

23

A better alternative is to use either all the same serif font or a combination of one serif font with one sans-serif font. Then there is enough contrast.

Serif Headlines Work With Sans-serif Text

Bold Subheads Can Be the Same Size as Text
Text can be in Roman or Light weight and the same size as subheads. The principle is to have as few type differentiators as your material will support. Remember SIMPLICITY is the soul of good design. Reserve the use of italics for *emphasis* within a block of text.

Sans-serif Headlines Work With Serif Text

Bold Subheads Can Be the Same Size as Text
Text can be in Roman or Light weight and the same size as subheads. The principle is to have as few type differentiators as your material will support. Remember SIMPLICITY is the soul of good design. Reserve the use of italics for *emphasis* within a block of text.

The same idea applies to large font families that contain condensed and extended variants. For instance, we should consider Helvetica Condensed or Helvetica Extended to be different typeface designs from Helvetica, because they are different font designs. The fundamental shapes of the letterforms have been changed. They can no longer coincide.

This does not apply to italic or boldface. Those are weight or emphasis alternatives within a single font and were created to be used together.

Within a layout, one single font, with only weight and size distinguishing headlines, subheads and text. Captions are usually offset from body text with only size to differentiate.

While using **bold** or *italic* in the same font are fine for emphasis, using alternate width variants poses the same problem: Not enough contrast but too different to coincide.

Coincide or Contrast in a Layout

Positioning elements is another way to apply the Coincide or Contrast principle. Unless there is a specific reason to do otherwise, aligning elements places the focus on the content and not the arrangement, which is as it should be. The purpose of design is to aid communication, not draw undue attention to itself. If elements are only slightly misaligned, it just looks like a mistake.

Now that we've laid a foundation by discussing a few basic principles of design, let's examine the actual subject of this book: Corporate Identity Design.

Chapter Two

Branding Fundamentals

A Brief Overview of Branding History

Branding design is not just a modern pursuit; it has been practiced from the dawn of civilization. Many different approaches have been used, some in media or materials that are not commonly used today. Each method and medium imposed certain constraints on designers.

Cuneiform is the oldest form of writing, dating from about 3000 BC. But even before that—as much as 500 years before—Mesopotamian cylinder seals were in use. These seals were a major inspiration for the development of writing. They were used to identify goods and sign contracts, and were considered so precious that they accompanied the dead in their tombs. Skilled craftsmen made them from hard stones, even gemstones such as hematite, obsidian, steatite, amethyst, lapis lazuli and carnelian. When rolled on soft clay, they left an imprint that was

Cylinder seals and the impressions they made in clay. Courtesy of the Louvre

the owner's brand. Their use was legally binding, much as signatures on legal documents are today.

Considering that, branding design predates even the invention of writing.

The Egyptians enclosed the names of their pharaohs in cartouches. These encapsulated names can also be thought of as the precursors of modern logos.

From ancient cultures as diverse as Egypt and China, royal seals not only signified royalty, but also were used to authenticate royal edicts, treaties and laws. This tradition has continued to modern nations, which use them the way corporations use logos.

1. Royal Seal of Pharoah Sahure, c2500 BC. 2. Egyptian Royal Seal Ring. 3. Imperial Royal Seal of the Great Han Empire c200 BC. 4. Impression from the Royal Seal of King Henry VIII of England. Courtesy Wikimedia Commons.

Japanese mon are family crests, and many have been unchanged for centuries. They were used as patterns on armor, flags, swords, clothing and other personal articles. By the 12th century AD, crests were widely used by aristocratic families, and since then were increasingly adopted by common folk. Many mon embody principles of modern logo design. The logo for the Mitsubishi Group is a combination of the family mon of the founder's family and the mon of his first employer's family.

European medieval heraldry provided identification on the battlefield, where helmets covered knights' faces. Specific symbols and color combinations were placed on helmet decorations, tunics and shields. Elaborate coat of arms designs evolved from these original, simpler designs. Only a single heir legitimately inherited the coat of arms. Non-inheriting sons had to create a new one, often variants of the original. We could consider these as proto-logos.

 Aketi
 Aoi
 Asahina
 Botan Chou
 Chigai Hishi
 Chigai Kuginuki
 Daki Myoka
 Fukushima

 Gamo
 Gion Mamori
 Gomaisasa
 Hanawachgai
 Hatakeyama
 Hoyo
ii
Inemaru Ni Ichi

 Ishikawa
 Janome-Shichiyo
 Kawari-Itadori
 Kikawa
 Kiyobucho
 Mai-Hou-Ou
 Marunidakituno
Matsu

 Mituaoi
 Mouri
 Musubi Kashiwa
 Nagagawake
 Naruse
 Oda
 Saigo
Saito

 Simikiri Hana
 Takanoha
 Toda
 Toyotomi
 Tsugaru
 Ume
 Yamanouchi
 Yotsume

Examples of Japanese Family Mons (family crest symbols). There are more than 5,000 such mons on historical record.

Photos by Roger Medley

Because few people could read in medieval times, signage often had to communicate without words either the nature or the name of a business. A blacksmith sign might show a hammer and anvil; a potter's sign, a mug and pitcher. People who ran taverns and inns tended to choose names that could be illustrated on a sign. This is another centuries-old branding tradition.

Silversmith trademarks, like trademarks from many different trade guilds, were protected by law, with severe penalties for misuse.

Guilds gained strength in various trades by about 1000 AD and enforced quality standards of work among their members, who marked their work to identify it. This is the origin of the term "trademark." Similar labelling is still practiced.

Producing trademarks in crafts such as silversmithing required considerable mastery. In all cases, it was specialized craftsmen who created identifying devices down through the ages, such as cylinder seals or seal rings.

It is conceivable that apprentices to these craftsmen in each age balked at the stringencies of their respective crafts and wished they could perform their

jobs without first mastering such hard-won disciplines. For instance, we can imagine that an apprentice for a cylinder-seal master might propose making seals out of wood instead of the typical hard and unyielding stones. Unfortunately, a wooden seal would not release the clay. Or perhaps a new apprentice might want to employ a fine-lined design "just to be different," only to find that the clay stuck in the little lines and didn't remain in the impression.

There is no getting away from the discipline of each craft. So it is with modern identity design. All around us, people are "designing" unsuitable logos and selling them to unsuspecting business owners, who soon find out

that the logos don't work when printed in a single color, or that printing costs are double what they could be. Some logos can't be perceived clearly from a distance and are therefore useless on a sign. Some can't be shown small on a computer screen because, when rendered through the screen's grid of pixels, they become "pixel mush."

There are ways to avoid these and other pitfalls. The first step is learning the principles of solid corporate-identity design.

Next we'll look at some successful brand designs to find out what they can teach us.

Evolution of Some High Profile Identities

Learning from Others

Nobody can live long enough to learn solely from making one's own mistakes and expect to have learned very much before dying. It is wiser to try to learn from the successes and mistakes of others. It is wiser to try to learn from the successes and mistakes of others. It's less painful and learning what works and what doesn't can happen much faster.

Corporate Logo Evolution

The identities of large companies have changed over time, almost always gravitating toward simpler, more elegant designs, and usually conforming to the core principles that will be discussed later in this book. Many companies have a long history of attempting to refine their identity. If we look at their progression from one identity to another and compare, we can see some consistent trends.

These companies have worked hard to get their respective identities just right. Each change represents not only the combined efforts of dozens, if not hundreds, of individuals, but also a massive expenditure of resources.

1901 1907 1909 1913

1941 1974 1981 1999

Texaco's identity has been trendy at times but simplicity and clarity win in the end.

THE WESTINGHOUSE ELECTRIC COMPANY

1886

1900

1921

1936

1960 (Paul Rand)

Here the progression is ever simpler, cleaner, more direct. Note that Westinghouse changed its logo every 15 to 25 years. Then Paul Rand designed a new logo for Westinghouse, and it has remained virtually unchanged since 1960. Why? Because identities that are designed according to core principles don't become dated.

Rather than becoming harder to recognize by being stylized, if done properly, images become clearer. Beginning with photo-like realism, these logos became increasingly stylized until Raymond Lowey made a perfect Shell logo in 1971. The typography, however, was too trendy and was replaced with a less dated font. Then in 1999 the company omitted the signature portion. Very few companies can ever do that.

1876	1912	1936	1937
1950	1956	1968	JOHN DEERE 2000

Through more than a hundred years of evolution, superfluous content is eliminated in the John Deere logo; realism is exchanged for stylization; elements are made simpler and more powerful.

The pre-Victorian first logo for Apple Computers didn't last even one year. The elegant apple logo was designed in 1976 by Rob Janoff. After that, the rainbow colors were omitted along with the trendy type (such type always goes out-of-date quickly). All the changes since then have been treatments; they have been supplemental to the basic flat color logo, but have never replaced it. Even today on the Apple website, it's the simple, one-color logo that is used, not the treatments.

What are the common design trends that these case studies show?

First and foremost, clarity and ease of recognition are paramount. These are absolute baseline requirements. Over and over, the designs prove one overriding principle: nothing can compensate for lack of clarity. Those who think that clarity is somehow passé are smoking something that's messing with their heads. Without legibility, nothing else matters. If people cannot see and recognize the brand, the design is a failure, pure and simple.

Next are twin qualities that are also indispensable in corporate-identity design: flexibility and continuity.

Over and over again we see that simplicity triumphs over complexity, one color over multiple colors, and timeless designs over trendy ones.

Great Designers of the Last Century

Some designers intuitively worked in harmony with the core principles. Their work, consequently, has stood the test of time. They can teach us much. Even the few times when they missed the mark can show us that these principles cannot be ignored.

Herb Lubalin, 1918-1981
Herb Lubalin was educated at Cooper Union. During his career he had an affinity for individually rendered typographic identities, which made him an ideal creator of magazine mastheads. Notable examples were the identities for three magazines co-published with Ralph Ginzburg: *Eros*, *Fact* and *Avant Garde*, where Lubalin also did the art direction, often using

full-page typographic titles. He created several notable type fonts, including Avant Garde, modeled after the magazine identity of the same name. He founded International Typographic Corporation (ITC) and left a lasting mark on the world of font design. A memorable publicity tool of ITC's was the free publication *U&lc* (Upper and Lower Case), where he spent the last ten years of his life. It was a showcase of eclectic typographic experimentation. Lubalin's work as a custom typographer often incorporated swashes and ligatures and has been a lasting example of exquisite wordmarks at their best, embracing both complexity and clarity.

Paul Rand, 1914-1996
Paul Rand was educated at Pratt Institute, Parsons, The New School for Design and the Art Students League but was mostly a self-taught designer. He built his early career on the strength of his page layouts, including his ability to crop photos for maximum impact. During his lifetime he was recognized for painting, lecturing and industrial design, but he is remembered today mostly for his world-famous logo designs.

As long as a half-century later, many of those brand designs remain essentially unchanged. He continued to be commissioned for high-level identity design into his eighties. More than any other individual of his era, Rand helped

Esquire Magazine
1938

IBM

IBM 1957

Harcourt Brace
1957

Consolidated Cigar
Corp 1959

Westinghouse
1960

UPS 1961

ABC 1962

Cummins 1962

Atlas Crankshaft
1964

IBM 1967
(13 bar variation)

IBM 1972
(8 bar variation)

Tipton Lakes
1980

Yale University
Press 1985

Connecticut Art
Directors Club 1986

Next 1986

IDEO 1991

Morningstar 1991

Osakan
Securities 1991

Education First
1993

Creative Media
Center 1994

USSB 1995

Enron 1996

Norwalk Cancer
Center 1996

big business understand the value of design and of taking graphic design beyond the mere creation of a logo – in fact, toward a holistic design philosophy. Some criticized his designs as simplistic, but his insight has been proven correct: to have a long life, a good design needs to be simple and restrained. Perhaps Rand's most famous logo is the IBM monogram, originally designed in 1957 and modified by him ten years later and again in 1972. It is interesting that each successive improvement corrected negative issues referred to later in this book. Even the few Rand logos that did not stand the test of time serve to underscore the core principles. No matter how famous you are, an identity that doesn't conform to the core principles will be less than effective and is likely to be replaced.

Saul Bass, 1920-1996

Saul Bass was another graphic designer whose identities have lasted decades without ever looking out-of-date or passé. His design credo was "symbolize and summarize," advice that is just as valid today.

After his education at the Art Students League (on a scholarship) and evening classes with György Kepes at Brooklyn College, Bass moved to Hollywood to work on print ads. He produced dozens of film titles for directors like Preminger, Hitchcock and Kubrick, and dozens of movie posters. He also did many book covers and made several small films, winning an Academy Award in 1968 for his film *Why Man Creates*.

Concurrent with his work in film, Bass distinguished himself in corporate design. Many of his logos remain virtually unchanged today, save for modest

variations and treatment alterations. The few logos that were abandoned were mostly victims of corporate mergers or cessations. When Bass's original designs were replaced, the new ones were almost always weaker and full of difficulties that will surely mean a shorter lifespan than that of their predecessors. When it comes to companies' retaining logos over time, Saul Bass has a better track record than Paul Rand. This should not be surprising because Bass's logos more consistently adhere to the core principles that we'll discuss later.

Lawry's Foods 1959

Fuller Paints 1962

Alcoa 1963

Celanese 1965

Security Pacific Bank 1966

Rockwell 1968

Continental Airlines 1968

Dixie 1969

AT&T Corporation 1969

Quaker Oats 1969

United Way 1972

United Airlines 1974

Warner Communications 1974

Avery 1975

Girl Scouts 1978

Minolta 1978

Wienerschnitzel 1978

Frontier Airlines 1981

AT&T 1983

US Postage 1983

Kibun Foods 1984

General Foods 1984

Kleenex 198?

NCR Corporation 1996

AT&T 1996

Walter Landor, 1913-1995
and Landor Associates
Born Walter Landauer in Munich, Germany, Landor moved to San Francisco, California, in 1939 and founded Landor Associates in 1941. The company has offices around the world. Educated in London before moving to the States, he became, at age 23, the youngest Fellow to date of the Royal Society of Arts. Landor and his company have designed hundreds of identities, including a number for airlines.

Many of these designs have stood the test of two to five decades: however, the less successful ones were replaced more quickly than those of any other designer in this section, perhaps because of their earlier tendency to use current or trendy typefaces, which soon become dated.

Delmonte
1963

Bank of America
1969

Levi Strauss
1969

Cotton
1973

Alitalia
1967

Hawaiian Airlines
1974

Thai Airlines
1975

Squirt
1978

Frito Lay
1979

Dole
1984

JAL 1989

US Air
1979

AirCal
1981

SAS
1983

Fuji Film
1987

Touchstone Pictures
1984

Garuda Indonesia
1985

British Airways 1984

Northwest Airlines
1989

Netscape
1994

World Wildlife
Federation 1988

Hyatt Hotels
1990

NEC
1992

Federal Express
1994

Chermayeff and Geismar

Ivan Chermayeff
born 1932
(still working)

Tom Geismar
born 1931
(still working)

Before joining forces, Chermayeff and Geismar were well educated in graphic design. They met at Yale, where Chermayeff earned a bachelor of fine arts and Geismar his master's degree.

Originally their firm was a threesome – Brownjohn, Chermayeff and Geismar. Robert Brownjohn left after two years. Since then, the firm has been responsible for more than one hundred identities for companies all over the world and has won virtually every award in the industry. While not all of their logo designs conform to the core principles, the most long-lived ones do. Note that although their logos are reproduced fairly small here, they are clear and solid; and even though they sometimes contain more than one color, each one would work in a single color.

Screen Gems

Merck
Pharmaceuticals

Embassy
Communications

Burlington
Industries

TechCommons

Seatrain Lines

Univision

Shotime Networks

Mobil Corporation

Smithsonian
Institution

Clay Adams

The American Film
Institute

Lincoln Center

New York
University

Owens-Illinois

Xerox

HarperCollins

PBS

Chase Manhattan
Bank

New School
University

JFK Presidential
Library

NBC

United States
Bicentennial

Koc Holding

Nippon Life

What does reviewing these famous designers' work teach us?

All of them created great identities. When they did miss the mark, the result reinforces the core principles.

Chapter Three

Core Principles

Generating Concepts

Corporate Identity Components

Four Identity Components

Before we try to generate concepts, let us stop to remember that there are four different kinds of corporate-identity design components. They are:

1) Signatures
2) Wordmarks
3) Monograms
4) Logos

Signatures

As the name implies, a signature is simply a unique way of writing a name. Similarly, brand signatures are corporate names written in a specific font, which may or may not be encapsulated in a simple geometric shape. They have no distinguishing or unique design element added; they are just the corporate name set in a particular font or style of lettering.

Signatures are often just a particular font used to spell the functional name of the company. They are the least value-added in corporate-identity design and are most often used for consumer products.

Signatures are best suited for brand-name consumer products and the corporations that produce them. Examples are: Alka-Seltzer, Sony, Epson, Daewoo, Clinique, Nintendo and Gillette. This is the most basic form of value-added design, and signatures alone are generally not well suited for identities of other kinds of businesses or corporations.

Originally, the term "signature" meant a personal, handwritten name with distinctive characteristics. Interestingly, a signature that is truly distinctive, with a deliberate and individual treatment of letters or a unique design element, is no longer properly called a signature, but a wordmark.

Some companies, even in the consumer product category, that formerly had signatures alone for their products have added something unique, such as a hand-lettered wordmark or a logo.

Wordmarks

Wordmarks are sometimes also called logotypes. But some people erroneously say logotypes or wordmarks when they mean signatures or logos. Therefore, because of misuse, the term logotype might well be avoided altogether. For our purposes, plain type "right off the keyboard" (with proper kerning, of course) does not constitute a wordmark; that's just a signature. A wordmark, on the other hand, must have some unique design element, perhaps just a type ligature.

The biggest drawback with wordmarks is that they have only one format, whereas both monograms and logos, because they are separated from their signatures, can be arranged in different configurations for varying layout needs.

Even so, wordmarks are, and will continue to be, very useful for corporate identity.

What distinguishes a wordmark from a signature is some unique design element.

Monograms

Monograms are a kind of logo that includes or resembles the initial(s) of the company's functional name. Monograms are most often used with an accompanying signature but sometimes appear alone (without the full corporate name contained in a signature), as in the case of IBM or NASA, where the initials have become the functional corporate name and not the words they originally stood for – for example, IBM for International Business Machines. Sometimes, as in the case of NASA (the National Aeronautics and Space Administration), the monogram becomes a coined word or acronym.

Monograms usually contain the first letter or letters of the corporate name rendered in a unique graphic way. The signature spells out the corporate name (Motorola and Hilton). Note that the signature font either contrasts in style with the monogram font (Motorola and Kawasaki) or matches it exactly (Chanel).

Similar but non-matching fonts don't work well. This is the principle of "coincide or contrast" that we have already addressed. Avoid making the monogram the first letter in the signature, as this often interferes with easy reading.

Monograms typically use the first initial(s) in the functional name. Unless they spell out the whole functional name, as they do with IBM and NASA, they usually also include a signature.

Logos

Logos are unique design elements that do not resemble letters. They are separate from, but usually used in conjunction with, a signature, type "right off the keyboard" (with proper kerning, of course), which usually has no distinctive design elements of its own. As with monograms, avoid using the logo in place of any letter in the signature.

Why This Book's Name?

Even though, for the purposes of this book, I assign separate terms for monograms and wordmarks, the population at large associates the word logo with anything that is used as a corporate identity. Hence, in that context, the title *Logo Theory* may be understood by the layman as well as the professional.

Functional Name versus Legal Name

In identity design, the full legal name is not used. Words such as "corporation," "company" or "Inc." are almost never included. Instead, a shorter name, often just one word, is the functional name used in either a signature or wordmark.

Recognizing that there are only four possible components serves both to t the design process and to help a designer cover all bases when developing ideas or concepts, which we'll cover next.

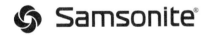

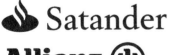

Logos are almost always accompanied by a signature.

Section 13

Identity Concepts: Corporate Activity

Design concept is quite different from the issue of identity components mentioned previously. Some people may be surprised to discover that, among the millions of existing different logos and corporate identities, there are only four basic categories of concepts. They are:

1) Corporate Activity
2) Corporate Ideals
3) Corporate Name
4) Abstract

Corporate Activity

These identities show something about the product or the activity of the company. The monogram for Westinghouse, which makes electrical and electronic appliances, is a W that resembles an electronic circuit. The monogram for Allied Van Lines is the letter A, made to resemble a two-lane highway, because Allied Van Lines moves your household belongings "down the road." The logo for tire manufacturer Uniroyal is a stylized tire on pavement. This kind of identity shows what a company does and is, perhaps the first thing that many beginning designers think of when developing identity concepts. It is a tried and true approach, but it is not the only kind of identity concept and not necessarily the best.

When developing new identity concepts, think of ways to visualize what a company does, and try to make from each concept a logo.

Then, see if each of your corporate activity concepts can be incorporated in the logical initial of the company name, making a monogram.

Corporate activity logos illustrate what the company does or makes.

Next, determine which combinations of activity concepts can be made with the whole word(s) of the functional corporate name. Here, different fonts will allow different possibilities, but avoid fonts that sacrifice clarity for decorative, stylistic or trendy considerations. They will become dated most quickly.

If you don't consider how each concept could be incorporated into each of the three possible components, many good possibilities will be left unexplored.

This is only one of the four possible conceptual approaches to a corporate identity. There are three more to follow.

Designers need to determine how the corporate activity can be visualized while being combined with the appropriate letterform, the first initial(s) of the functional name.

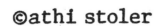

Wordmarks with a corporate activity concept.

45

Section 14

Identity Concepts: Corporate Ideals

Instead of showing what a company does, these identities visualize something about the qualities or ideals to which the company aspires. This can be ideals such as "superiority," "strength," "speed," or "accuracy."

The important thing to remember is that these ideals may not be obvious to the public when viewing the logo but can act subliminally. People don't have to say, "Gee that makes me think of protection and someone taking care of me." But a logo that has a band around something may communicate that on an unconscious level.

Occasionally a double entendre will occur with an identity communicating more than one thing. Those times are serendipitous but trying for multiple concepts can ruin an identity. Doing one thing well is always better than doing two things poorly.

Harris Bank uses a lion, "king of the jungle," for superiority and leadership. Merrill Lynch stockbrokers' logo uses a stylized bull since a bull market is a prosperous, growing market, a very appropriate ideal to associate with a stock brokerage. The Prudential insurance logo is a stylized drawing of the Rock of Gibraltar, a symbol of permanence; their company slogan is, "As steady as the Rock of Gibraltar." Other ideals might be "love," "softness," "speed" or "fun."

Corporate ideals monograms. A shield can communicate strength or protection; arrows can show action; slanting letters can demonstrate speed. Can you see the skinny B inside the fat B? Other ideals shown here are movement, tranquility, friendship, healing, and new beginnings.

Corporate ideals wordmarks. Round edges can convey "safe for children"; odd shapes can say "fun"; straight horizontal lines can show motion.

Identity Concepts: Corporate Name

These identities do not show either corporate activity or ideals, but the name of the company itself. This approach will work only with certain corporate names.

Wendy's hamburger restaurants do not serve burgers made from little girls, nor does a little girl represent a particular ideal for the company. Instead, the Wendy's logo represents the company's namesake, the daughter of founder Dave Thomas. Petroleum does not come from decomposed sea shells, but Shell Oil's logo is a shell, representing its name. The corporate logo of Apple, the largest technology company in the world, is an apple, which has nothing to do with either computers or an ideal. Greyhound bus lines, John Deere farm machinery and Whirlpool appliances all use identities visualizing the corporate name directly. Of course, the very shapes of these designs must also be harmonious with corporate ideals and goals, but the logo comes primarily from the name.

These logos generally do not depict the activity or the ideals of their companies, but rather the company name alone.

Interestingly, there are few occasions where the initials of a company's functional name can be described visually. Visually representing a name in combination with a monogram should be no harder than other concept/component combinations, but for some reason, good examples of monograms that show the corporate name seem to be quite rare.

Even though a corporate name logo or wordmark isn't meant to show ideals of the company directly, the style of drawing needs to be compatible with corporate ideals. The greyhound isn't sitting, but running. The apple logo is drawn with precision, not haphazardly or casually.

Corporate name wordmarks

49

Identity Concepts: Abstract

Some identities show nothing about the activities, ideals or even the names of their respective companies, but are designed with unique graphic or typographic treatments. Chrysler's five-pointed star inside a pentagram has nothing to do with cars. Neither does Chevrolet's parallelogram. Exxon's wordmark with interlocked "Xs" demonstrates no corporate activity, ideals or name. And there's no particular message in Disney's wordmark. All of these are abstract.

Even without the psychological ties of the other three conceptual approaches, abstract identities can be effective. However, the shapes of abstract identities must still be harmonious with the nature of the company and its ideals.

Now that we've covered the three possible identity components and four possible concept approaches, what do we do with this information?

Abstract Logos

Litton
 HUBBARD
 McCULLOCH
 Delco

 weyel international

 DAK
 TRW
 GM

 UNIVISION

 HEWLETT PACKARD
 MAYTAG

Abstract Monograms

EXXON   EXCEL.   TYCO   Allstate®   VOX

INTERPLAK   Liquitex®   Ford   USLIFE   Oster

NYNEX   FedEx®   AMETEK   THERMOS

digital   Mobil    SHERWIN Williams   USWEST

Alitalia   makita   case    Sunbeam

Abstract Wordmarks

Section 17

Knowing Your Client

You will create your best designs when you understand your client's needs— and even better, when you understand the needs of your client's customers, because they are the real audience. It is necessary in our profession for a designer to become an "instant expert" in various companies. This is a challenge, but it is also one of the perks. How can you get bored when you must think like an accountant one day, an industrialist the next and a service worker after that? For a designer of corporate identities, it's never "same old, same old."

But this "inside" knowledge doesn't come without effort. The easiest way to learn it is from your client.

Interviewing Your Client

Here is a sample of questions that can help you apply the four conceptual approaches:

• What is this company's activity?
• Specifically, what do you do? What is the essence of this business?
• What is the product of your business? What do your customers get from you (if a service business)?
• What objects or images can be associated with your company's products/services?
• What are the major competitors for your business or alternatives for your customers?

• What niche or characteristic makes your company unique?
• What qualities, feelings or ideals would your company like associated with it? (see Discovering Appropriate Ideas Activity)
• What sort of imagery could convey those ideals?
• What qualities, feelings or ideals would your company NOT want associated with it?
• What sort of images could be associated with your corporate name?
• What kinds of imagery are compatible with your company's character and specialties?
• What kinds of shapes are harmonious with the company's desired niche, character, specialties and ideals?
• How do you want your business to grow?
• What kind of clientele do you want to attract? Will this be a new market or greater share of your existing market?

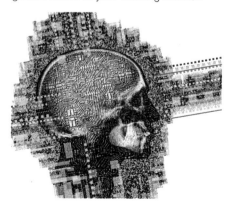

Is it domestic, business, industrial, international?

• What are some of the jargon words used in this industry for things like the customer's problem, a job well done, and so on?

• Comments / Questions / Clarifications

Discovering Appropriate Ideals

As part of a designer's interviewing of a client, the following exercise may be helpful. This will obviously inform corporate ideals concepts but will also help the designer choose shapes for executing any concept.

1. From the list of words in the following block, underline any word that should be associated with this company.

2. Put a box around any qualities with which your company would avoid association.

3. Go back through the list and circle the five that are or should be the most important definers of this company's identity.

4. It is quite likely that by going through the following list of words, other words that may be more appropriate for your client will emerge. Feel free to add words at the bottom of the grid that better fit qualities or ideals that your company would, or would not, want to be associated with.

Ideals Words

expansion	coalescing	divergence	movement	focus
open	strength	speed	accuracy	random
serious	juvenile	easy	difficult	solid
soft	professional	fluid	fun	technical
caring	strong	durability	educational	love
outward	inward	protective	steady	concluding
communication	contemporary	liberal	conservative	modest
coming together	beginning	purity	leadership	natural
economical	rich	traditional	contemporary	smart
feminine	masculine	casual	responsible	growing
protective	exciting	becoming	entertaining	healthy
illuminating	royal	achievement	activity	adaptability
consistent	in command	competitive	connectedness	analytical
fairness	finding	context	deliberate	discipline
development	empathy	futuristic	harmony	creativity
inclusive	individualistic	input	old fashioned	intelligence
maximum	positivity	relating	restorative	security
strategic	healthy	economical	first-class	caring
superior	friendly	exact	honest	reliable
_____	_____	_____	_____	_____
_____	_____	_____	_____	_____

Self-Brainstorming

Brainstorming

This is a term coined by advertising executive Alex F. Osborn for group co-operation in generating ideas. Three basic principles govern successful brainstorming:

1. All judgement is deferred to later.
2. Idea quantity is the goal.
3. Unusual ideas are valued, as are combined ones.

For this to work in a group, no one comments verbally or otherwise on any idea expressed. All ideas are recorded. This maxim prevails: "Quantity Breeds Quality." It is only later that the ideas are evaluated or sorted critically.

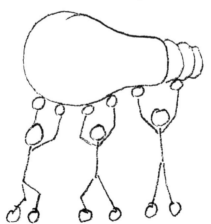

Ideas can come from many quarters. Since getting each and every idea drawn is essential, our stick men here are particularly appropriate.

One successful variation on this technique is called directed brainstorming. Each participant is asked to write one idea on a piece of paper. The papers are shuffled and exchanged, and each participant is asked to come up with a new idea that improves on the one already on the sheet. Participants again swap pages, and add improvements for another few rounds.

We'll look at these techniques and see how they apply to generating corporate identity concepts.

Left Brain, Right Brain

It is a popular notion that the two hemispheres of the human brain have divergent capabilities and inclinations, in addition to controlling opposite sides of the body. Generally speaking, the left side is credited with being the analytical, verbal/linguistic and logical side of the brain. The right side is thought to be the spatial, visual and creative side. Typically, the belief is that both sides can't work on their respective specialties at the same time.

Modern brain research does not support this concept. Instead, it shows that capabilities like speaking are dependent on various specific areas of the brain, each with different contributions to the whole process. It also shows that most processes are not exclusively left-brain or right-brain functions. While the pop

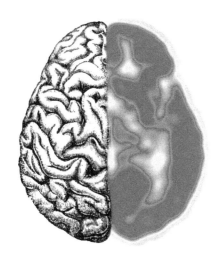

It's not an accurate model, but the left brain/ right brain image is useful for this exercise.

wisdom about left and right brains isn't completely true, the idea that different parts of our brains do different things is validated.

With that caveat in mind, and still using the model that the right side of the brain is the creative side, we might suppose that conceptualizing and designing corporate identities should be largely a right-brain activity, right?

Wrong.

Why would we think that half a brain could do a better job than a whole brain? Is there a way to get multiple parts of our brains working together synergistically?

Yes.

Visualize the four kinds of identity concepts as an outer ring of a wheel that can revolve around an inner circle that contains the three kinds of identity components. You can use this wheel to generate more ideas. Each identity component can work with any of the four identity concepts.

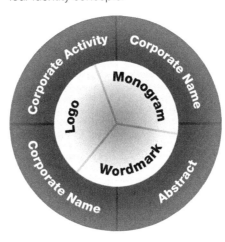

Since signatures have no concept at all other than font choice, they don't show on the inner circle (but are still needed to accompany a logo or a monogram).

You should try to have at least one or two of each of the following combinations:

- Corporate Activity Logos
- Corporate Ideals Logos
- Corporate Name Logos
- Corporate Activity Monograms
- Corporate Ideals Monograms
- Corporate Name Monograms
- Corporate Activity Wordmarks
- Corporate Ideals Wordmarks
- Corporate Name Wordmarks

Rather than the left brain getting in the way of the right brain, one side can act as a catalyst for the other. Instead of stifling creativity, this approach can promote it. Correctly practiced, this kind of conceptualizing can put any designer in the position of working from a wealth of good concepts. Instead of trying to come up with a single good idea, the designer might have to decide which of the good ones is the best. That's where we all want to be.

As you consider each idea, write it down and draw a quick thumbnail to record it. Every idea, not just the "good" ones. By considering each of the four different kinds of concepts, you are getting the left side of your brain to collaborate with or jump-start the right side. Later, every thumbnail or sketch can also help pollinate new ideas.

Working the Technique

Be sure to take notes when interviewing your client. Single words or phrases can be crucial. After reviewing your interview notes, ask yourself the same questions, but don't be content only with the client's answers. An experienced set of outside eyes may see things that the client doesn't. So when you ask yourself the following questions, see if you can come up with the most accurate and useful answers.

- What is this company's activity?
- Specifically what does it do?
- What is the essence of the business?
- What objects or images can relate this company's products or services?
- What niche (such as quality, speed or price) makes this company different from its competitors?

Ask yourself all the questions you asked the client and put your answers, if different, in a different color in the margins of your client notes. Compare them. Try to articulate why you had any different answers. Note those things too.

Some of the answers may lend themselves to more than one of the conceptual approaches. For instance, something might be interpreted as the company's activity or the company's ideals. It doesn't matter what slot it gets categorized in. What matters is that the

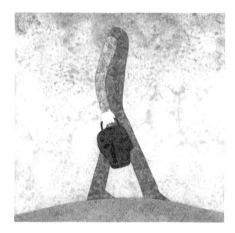

concept was generated, and became a tangible idea.

Make written lists of objects that can represent, or be associated with, the corporate activity. Make initial sketches of those objects.

Then take it a step further. Think how these concepts might be shown in a less-than-literal way. Some designers tend to be too realistic in producing an image. Logos are not illustrations and certainly not clip art. Back off. Instead of being confined by a literal likeness, try to merely suggest the object in question. Many of the best corporate activity identities have this less-than-literal quality.

Next, consider ideals that the client might legitimately aspire to or, conversely, which qualities or ideals

might be antithetical to the client's image. After determining the top five company ideals, think of ways to represent them. What symbols might you use? A lion can represent superiority or royalty as well as strength. A flower can represent love, freshness, growth. Lines slanting to the right or arrows can mean forward motion and speed. Hearts, eagles and crowns are all images that communicate ideals. There are thousands of possibilities.

Is there a way to visualize the company name, perhaps with a mascot? Many company names are family names of the founder, but often those surnames have meanings that could be visually represented. Sometimes the logo can show how to pronounce the company name (such as the bear profile logo for Behr Paint). Always look up a company name in the biggest dictionary possible or an online dictionary that will define non-English words as well. Wikipedia has entries on a surprising range of words.

The term "abstract" conveys a lack of associations. That doesn't mean that any old image will necessarily work for a given logo. What graphic shapes are naturally compatible with the corporate activity or ideals without actually representing them? The Chevrolet logo doesn't look like a car but has been a very effective abstract logo for more than a century.

You haven't done a complete exploration of conceptualizing until you have come up with a few ideas associated with each of the four identity concepts on the outside of the wheel, combined with each of the three components on the inside. It may be difficult to apply your brain to each combo, but the exercise will bear fruit, be assured.

In effect, this technique allows you to brainstorm with yourself. During a proper multi-person brainstorming session, evaluations are not allowed. The object is to get as many ideas as possible on the table or on paper and do the sorting later. It should be the same for you at

this stage. Resist the temptation to evaluate while in the act of generating ideas. Let the flow happen.

Sketch every idea. No slacking. Don't edit or evaluate. Later, a poor idea might just have a shape or an element that will be the key to a truly memorable design. Original image courtesy Tolga Kocak. Freepik.com

Evaluating from a Position of Plenty

With a basket full of ideas, the designer can turn off the idea stream and put on a different hat. Now each idea can be examined. If a single concept seems inadequate, see if two concepts can be merged, as long as the concepts are compatible. Even those ideas that may look useless, overused or trite, in combination with some other element, may become a truly remarkable design.

With some practice, this technique will produce several good ideas, from which the very best can be selected. Conversely, designers who stop at one or two ideas cannot afford to evaluate them too closely because they have not developed the ability to generate ideas on demand. But when generating ideas no longer is a major hurdle, attention can then be directed to developing the greatest ones instead of adequate ones.

Two Warnings:

1. Don't conceptualize on the computer. Use a pencil for quick sketching.

2. Later, when combining and refining ideas, don't draw in lines but in solid shapes. This will be understood better after we discuss the Seven Deadly Sins of Logo Design.

Chapter Four

Core Principles

Seven Deadly Sins of Logo Design

Blowout

Use of Branding

For most readers of this book, the word branding conjures up images of logos, ads and labels. But agricultural branding of cattle practiced today is millennia old. It didn't start with cowboys in the Wild West; it dates all the way back to ancient Egypt. Not only was its purpose the same as it is today—to identify whose cow was whose—but the nature of those brands was similar to modern cattle brands. They had to be relatively simple, and they had to be easily recognized.

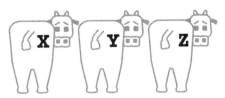

The purpose of a cow brand is similar to a brand or corporate identity in modern marketing:
to identify the owner.

Imagine a dude who has gone out West to be a cowboy. He designs a new brand for his cows that's unlike any of the others being used—"just to be different." The oldtimers tell him the brand won't work, but he doesn't listen. The young dude answers, "You're just jealous because my brand is distinctive, innovative, ahead of its time. Well, isn't

What good is a cow brand that can't be distinguished from a few feet away, if the design is obscured by nearby hair or when the cow is wet?
Photo courtesy of Searle Ranch.

that the whole purpose of a brand, to be unique?"

So this dude goes ahead and brands all his cows with his new "innovative" brand design. But the shapes are so fine that the nearby hairs disguise the brand. And when it rains, and the cow gets wet, it can't be seen at all.

Yes, it is new and different, but it isn't a very good brand design, is it?

"Just don't drive it in the rain. Don't take more than two people in it at a time. Oh, and the brakes don't work in cold weather. Aside from that, it's a great car."

Or imagine you are considering buying a used car and the salesman says something like this, "Just don't drive it in the rain. Don't take more than two people in it at a time. Oh, and the brakes don't work in cold weather. Aside from that, it's a great car!" You would probably shop elsewhere.

Lazy Design

The idea that lack of a little care can lead to big disaster isn't new. The centuries-old proverb "For the Want of a Nail" is a perfect example of a small consideration having large consequences.

> For want of a nail,
>   the shoe was lost;
> For want of a shoe,
>   the horse was lost;
> For want of a horse,
>   the rider was lost;
> For want of a rider,
>   the message was lost;
> For want of the message,
>   the battle was lost;
> For want of a battle,
>   the kingdom was lost.
> All for the want
>   of a horshoe nail.

If the proverbial nail was missing due to abject poverty, it would be unfortunate. If it was just wear and tear, we could chalk it up to fate. But if the missing nail was an act of carelessness, then it is truly tragic.

Too many designers don't know the serious errors that can be made in identity design. But even worse, some don't care. They don't care that the client won't get full utility out of the identity they've designed. For them, the pursuit of cool trumps the creation of an effective identity.

That's lazy design.

Design isn't brilliant because it's different; it's brilliant if it works beautifully in all situations.

Sadly, our design publications are filled with identities that are touted as being new and different but will utterly fail at their fundamental purpose—being seen and recognized or being reproduced in a variety of situations. No wonder so many designers today have no clue what good identity design is.

One of our original premises in this book is that a professional always acts in the client's best interests. Therefore, a designer's first responsibility is to create an identity design that will meet all the requirements necessary: to be clear, recognizable, and reproducible and consistent on all of the client's desired presentations—signage, vehicles, business forms, ads or websites.

Imagine a designer meeting with a client to present an identity and, after unveiling the design, says, "This is a cool design, but people will have a hard time seeing it on your vehicles. And you'll need to make it at least an inch-and-a-half tall on your website for good clarity. Oh, and by the way, it won't photocopy or fax well at all. And forget about it looking good in the Yellow Pages."

Sound far-fetched?

Sad to say, thousands of clients have paid so-called professional designers for work that has just those kinds of limitations. The worst part is that neither the clients (understandably) nor the designers (shamefully) had enough foresight to predict this.

Let's take this in a different direction. How many holes can your car's gas tank have before it's a threat? (And we're not talking about the input line or the fuel line to the engine, either.) How many holes can a balloon have before it pops? How many holes can a tire have before it has a blowout?

The correct answer in all three cases is "just one." It takes only one hole in each situation to pose a serious problem.

Too many who claim the title of designer have no clue what their "lack of a nail" will cause. A poorly designed identity could double or triple certain reproduction costs. It could simply not work on signage or when the identity has to be used small. It could reflect poorly on the client because of sloppy rendering. It could just be insipid and weak.

Seven Deadly Sins

It may strike some as overly melodramatic to use the term Seven Deadly Sins to describe shortcomings in logo design. Perhaps so. However, our look at the history of several corporate identities shows us that companies will and do get rid of identities that don't serve well. Sometimes it's due to corporate takeovers or other changes in corporate structure, but more often these companies simply realize that the current identity just "doesn't work" in one or more situations. Given the massive expenditure that revising a corporate identity represents, smart companies obviously want a corporate identity that always "works." Trial and error does eventually get better results, but it's a terribly lengthy and expensive process.

Photo courtesy TireZoo.com

Wouldn't it be easier to look at other people's mistakes and simply avoid those same mistakes? Some feel that such restrictions stifle their creativity, but if the goal is to get somewhere, why not take the route with the fewest pitfalls and dead ends?

I propose that there are indeed seven errors in identity design that are like that fatal hole in the balloon or the tire. If any identity doesn't work in the way it should, it's busted.

It's broken.

It's a blowout.

Section 20

Deadly Sin of Logo Design #1:

Can't Work In Black Only

Every identity ought to be able to work in one single flat color, like black. Even if black isn't the official "corporate" color, if the design doesn't work in black, it doesn't work.

Too many think this has no relevance today. They think that, in this day of computer graphics and the Web 2.0 look, such notions are archaic and passé. But lest I come across as a grumpy design curmudgeon with backward or retro ideas, look at the innovators of that very Web 2.0 look. What company has led the way in industrial design and digital utility more than any other? What company epitomizes contemporary design and

refinement in everything from advertising to packaging to product design?

Apple.

Some might ask, "Doesn't Apple have a logo that employs that cool transparent glass or jelly look?" Yes, but it is based on a solid black design. In fact, the company still uses the solid shape—not the Web 2.0 version—on all its products. Go to the Apple website. Do you see the transparent jelly version of the Apple logo anywhere? No. In fact, how big is their logo? Only 21 pixels high! Try doing that with a logo whose *only* version has a color jelly or transparent look.

Once you have a solid, well-designed identity, you can always embellish it. Each of these logos is based on a solid shape. There's no problem embellishing a solid shape. But the reverse is not always true: if you start with the multicolored, 3D, or transparent version, you may find nothing substantial under all the visual adornment.

The logo in the navigation masthead from the Apple website. On many pages, this is the only logo Apple uses, and only 21 pixels high!

The issue isn't that the glass look is wrong. It's just that the transparent or dimensional look is not where you start. You start with a solid design, and add the whistles and bells afterward. You don't design something that is all whistles and bells but has no substance. You can always embellish a solid design. But when you start with an embellishment, there may not be a solid design underneath it.

Regrettably, too many identities are designed this way, and not just for companies that couldn't afford the best design. Ignorance about this principle is rampant in the graphic design industry today.

Photographs and illustrations do not make for good logos or identities. There are too many subtleties that just don't translate into different media and at the sizes where a properly designed logo should be able to survive. Photographs can't be reproduced faithfully in cut vinyl for vehicles and signage. One might counter that we now can reproduce photos in vinyl. True, but at an increased cost, and they don't last as long as cut vinyl. But even more common

Here we see some recent multi-color illustrations masquerading as logos. After taking away all the color, most of them are wimpy at best. When you render them in black only, as in a photocopy, they are almost unrecognizable. Sadly, most of these were featured in design annuals as good examples of logo design. They are not.

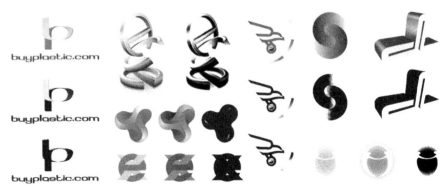

Gradients may disguise the inherent weaknesses of certain designs. How many of these have the internal contrast to provide excellent legibility? Rendered in solid black, they fail altogether.

processes, like photocopying, will compromise the clarity of a photo or illustration masquerading as a logo.

Some designers think gradients are acceptable for identity design, reasoning that halftones will reproduce them well. That is true for magazines and brochures, where the printing quality is relatively high, but what of the smaller printing presses used for most companies' stationery reproduction? Beyond that, newspapers and the Yellow Pages do poorly with halftones. Because of their poorer paper quality, a coarser dot-per-inch halftone is often used where gradients can end up looking blotchy.

Color is a beautiful thing, but even when using flat colors in identity design, multiple colors can be a mask that hides the lack of a fully developed core design. Too many colors can be a crutch. Ask yourself, "Can the design walk without the crutch of color?" Design implies finished forms, not half-baked shapes that must have the color to work. If it doesn't work in black only, it doesn't work.

There are many media, such as magazine ads, internet, TV and packaging, full color is a given, with no extra cost for a multi-color identity. But in many other formats—including stationery, everyday business forms, signs and vehicle identification—needing to show a multi-color identity will significantly increase costs by 150 per cent, 300 per cent or even 400 per cent. Persuading clients to buy into those extra costs, without having warned them beforehand, is extremely unprofessional.

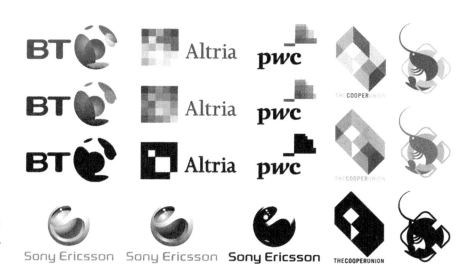

Losing the crutch of color, can these logos walk on their own? Some limp along; some fall flat.

It is amazing how often this happens. Clients may not think of the reproduction difficulties that a particular logo design can present. That is not their job. But it *is* the designer's job to think ahead and to be professional enough to give clients a choice.

Very few multicolored designs are so wonderful that an alternative design that works as well in black only would not have been preferable.

Every identity design ought to be able to work in a single flat color.

Section 21

Deadly Sin of Logo Design #2:
Lack of Mass

Mass gives an identity visibility at a distance or in small sizes. The shapes that make up the identity should not be lightweight or thin. An identity with insubstantial and flimsy parts is ineffectual and feeble.

Some diehards will suggest that contemporary identities can break older rules in the name of being modern. Now I ask: aren't websites modern? The bottom-right corner of the illustration here shows lines that are supposed to be black but are so thin that none of the pixels of the logo are a genuine black,

nor even close to it. This is a problem I call "Pixel Mush." Thin elements and lines do not display clean shapes when viewed through a grid of pixels. Far from liberating lazy designers from old constraints, the Web adds new ones of its own.

I propose a small experiment. For this, you will have to practice using what I call a "cold eye," which means to look at things as if you had never seen them before. Ask yourself, "If I did not already know what these images are, could I tell now?" That's using a cold eye.

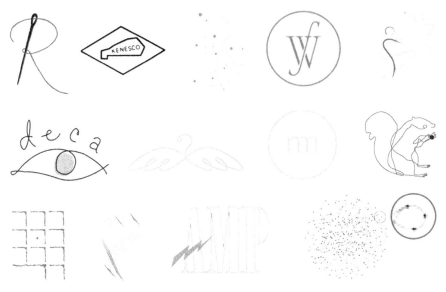

All of these suffer from lack of mass. Some are compounded by being in mid- or light-mid colors. The logo in the bottom-right corner has difficulty on the Web because the lines are so thin they have to be made up of pixels that are not black, even though the line is supposed to be black. That's what I call "Pixel Mush."

Now look up a page of logos by one of the great masters of design, Paul Rand or Saul Bass (Section 11). Or if those two are too historical for you, look up the logos of Chermayeff and Geismar, who are still alive and producing identities for major companies all around the globe. Stand back several feet. See how far you can go before being unable to discern the individual designs of the great logo designers. Then look at the logos above, at the same distance, and with a cold eye. Can you see the problem now? By comparison, they are barely discernible.

One large and famous New York design studio has dozens of high-profile identity designs to its credit. Here is a black-and-white poster from the studio's own website that displays 458 logos. Many of them are good, serviceable identities. But notice how some are recessive and hard to discern because of lack of mass. This is particularly true of some of the typographic identities. If they don't have a certain minimum amount of mass, they are hard to see. They're wimpy.

Some designs have two different values—in other words, not solid black only (Deadly Sin of Logo Design #1). I rest my case.

Please note that I did not alter this image. It is taken directly from the studio's own website, pixel-for-pixel, yet it demonstrates how breaking either of

Shown here are 458 identities created by a famous design studio in New York. This image is pixel-for-pixel as it appeared on their own website. Note that many identities have no mass and consequently are hard or impossible to discern.

these two Deadly Sins is, indeed, fatal to producing a legible identity – even if you are a famous designer.

Some may observe that what works on the Web at a nominal 72 pixels per inch will not convert to print, where 300 pixels per inch is the standard. True. Others may claim that the logos shown here are so small that it is unreasonable to expect them to be legible. But some of the logos do very well in spite of the small size. Therefore, to allay any fears that I have cited a sample that doesn't properly apply, I also found on the same company's website many much larger logos and reproduced them here at 300 pixels per inch. The principle still holds true: identities without mass do not project themselves as well as those with mass. Some don't show up for other reasons, such as failing to work in black only. And some have visual difficulties for reasons that will be covered in upcoming Deadly Sins.

This principle of needing mass also applies to the typographic elements, but we will come back to those issues later.

Two Deadly Sins down. Five to go.

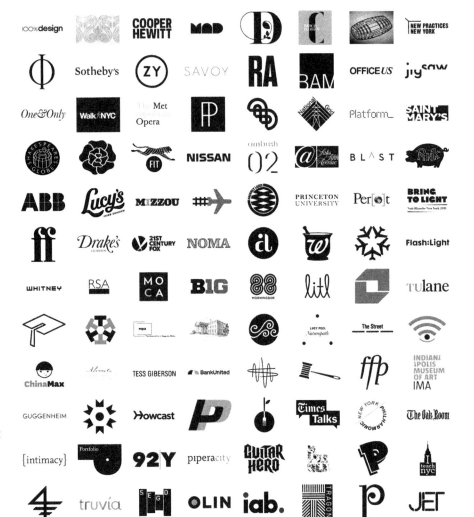

Even with the same studio's logos shown bigger (in the order they appear on the website), those that are without mass, or that need multiple values (Deadly Sin #1), suffer from less legibility.

Deadly Sin of Logo Design #3:

Obscure Contrast

Legibility is readability, the capacity to be correctly perceived or clearly deciphered. Legibility is a function of contrast. And contrast is a function of value. It doesn't matter so much what the hue or saturation is in the colors. What matters most for contrast is sufficient difference in value.

Any logo that has low contrast – and therefore low legibility – has failed its very reason for being: to be clearly seen and read.

There are two major kinds of contrast, and they are both essential for a good corporate identity: external contrast and internal contrast.

External contrast means having a good value difference between the design and the background. Internal contrast means that the logo elements can be distinguished from one another. A good identity has both.

This is another drawback to using gradients. In one area there may be sufficient contrast, but in others not.

One recurring pitfall that some designers fall into is trying to use all three of the

Some of these have poor contrast on a white background. Some have poor internal contrast. The old Family Channel logo had poor contrast on both light and dark backgrounds because the designer insisted on using the primary colors.

primary colors in an identity. It never
works. Yellow is a very light color,
and consequently will not show up
well against a white background.
Most shades of blue are too dark to
show up against a dark background.
Red is usually a mid-value color and
will not show up against a mid-value
background. Therefore, any identity that
uses all three primary colors risks having
some part fail to show up, no matter
what color background is used. It is one
of those "great ideas" that isn't great
after all.

A designer can sculpt the most exquisite
shapes with the best proportions and
then ruin the design by choosing colors
that give poor contrast.

Sounds like a blowout, doesn't it?

Deadly Sin of Logo Design #4:

Wayward or Parts Out of Harmony

Visual conflict – elements that don't harmonize—is another big pitfall in identity design. Because there are so many different manifestations of this particular deadly sin, we will look at numbered examples.

Slapping a shape on some letters without considering the relative contours is another all-too-common kind of lazy design (1).

Sometimes elements are not compatible or are mismatched in some manner. Here (5) we have a baroque-style illustration (we already have identified illustrations as a problem) together with type from the 1960s and '80s.

Another kind of disparity happens when designers try to create their own type (4). Most designers do not have the typographic skill to pull this off, and the results will usually look amateurish.

Rarely does using a logo as the first letter in the signature work well (7, 10, 11). It disrupts the easy reading of the signature. It's even worse if the logo is used for some letter in the middle of a signature (3, 9). If the letter is the same size as the other letters but very different in design, there is a discontinuity in reading the signature, and the word seems split in two.

1.

2.

3.

4.

5.

6.

7.

8.

9.

10.

11.

Treating letters in a single word in different graphic styles or colors (8) is also disruptive to reading the word; is it two words or one? The same disruption happens when some letters are a different size. Generally, it is better to keep the logo separate from the signature (6). Otherwise, just design a cohesive wordmark to begin with.

Yet a different kind of wayward design is when the mood or imagery are at odds with a professional image that befits the company. This can happen in many different ways but often it is a question of the design shapes reminding the viewer of something not intended or promoting association with incompatible ideals. Specific note on #2: Are those people in silhouette or bird droppings? What company would want that association?

Finally, a design that shows a double-entendre is a serendipitous delight, but when two or more concepts are forced together poorly or in an overly contrived manner, the result is a disastrous hodgepodge (3, 5, 7). This is akin to using every spice you have in a stew: garlic, cinnamon, thyme, peppermint and cayenne all together.

Deadly Sin of Logo Design #5:

Overlapping Elements

Overlapping was once a popular technique in identity designs, but people learned more than a hundred years ago that it reduces clarity.

Placing type over an image makes both the image and the type harder to read. Similar to overlapping is the practice of placing the signature inside

Each of these companies learned for themselves that overlapped elements don't work well and have abandoned them. Type is either subordinated inside the logo or legibility is compromised—or both.

1.
2.
3.
4.
5.
6.
7.
8.
9.
10.
11.
12.
13.
14.
15.

a visual element, which makes the type subordinate to the visual and reduces legibility. When the signature type is very brief, it can work, but only marginally. Larger signatures suffer considerably from this method. It should be avoided.

Overlapping causes conflicts between visual components and text or makes the text too small. For instance, in the Conte's identity (9), did you notice the words "MARKET & GRILL" in the upper fin and "WESTPORT" in the lower fin? Didn't think so.

Sometimes overlapping with lighter elements can be survived (2) but the text is not made easier to read by doing so. Drop shadows usually cut down on legibility.

Overlapping often involves placing text on top of a busy background (5, 6, 7, 11, 13), which makes the text difficult or nearly impossible to read (see Busy Backgrounds in Section 7).

Placing the logo in the middle of a two-word signature (14) disrupts the reading of the signature. Then, separating it from the signature for a different layout

becomes a breach of design continuity. Best to not do it at all.

Even in a relatively clear logo like Best Buy, the words were always subordinate to the label shape. In its improved new design, the Best Buy logo is separate from the signature and the whole identity is cleaner.

Capital One, on the other hand, has fixed the word "One" that was in a poorly contrasting gray, but improved nothing by adding a hackneyed swoosh shape that intersects the signature, making it harder to read.

Often the motivation to overlap identity elements is little more than an attempt to camouflage uninspired, lackluster or mismatched elements (8).

As with any other action that lessens clarity, overlapping elements should be avoided. It may not be a total disaster, but it *never* improves legibility. Instant clarity and readability are indispensable qualities of successful corporate identity.

Deadly Sin of Logo Design #6:

Unrefined Shapes

Vector art is the medium in which all identities should be created, but it can be deceptive. Vector art can give the impression that shapes are better than they are because the edges are crisp and clean. But shapes can be clean and sharp without being well rendered or refined. This can be especially true when altering letterforms (1, 2, 7) if the designer fails to be sensitive to the inherent shapes of the font. Something about Intel's logo must have bothered the company because they have replaced the design.

Lack of sensitivity to angles is another common shortcoming. In (4) the angles of the "f" are not the same as the angles of the containing box, neither coinciding nor contrasting. Irregular gaps between elements of (5) are laughable, not to mention the clumsy treatment of the

letters themselves. And speaking of poorly rendered letterforms, (12) is obviously not a properly rendered type design.

Curves also demand sensitive execution. Initially they can look passable, but on further consideration we notice that subtle sensitivities are missing. Over time these clumsy curves become irksome and grating (3, 9, 10). With curves, our eyes are coaxed into following a particular sweep. If the trajectory deviates from the anticipated course, it is disruptive. If it is overt and explicit, it becomes a focal point. If it is merely an unskilled deviation, it is a mark of amateur drawing. Note the inept curves in (9) and how curves are not even attempted in the bottoms of the sails.

Surprisingly, this lack of refinement is found in trademarks of some otherwise well-respected companies.

Here we come to a principle I call Visual Logic. Everything you draw sets up a visual expectation for the rest. For instance, in a series of uniform structures, one element that is slightly atypical will stick out like the proverbial sore thumb. If the difference is deliberate, overt and skillfully done, it becomes a point of emphasis. If it is not, it just comes across as ineptitude and clumsiness. In (11) the thickness of the straight lines is close, but not the same as those of the containing circle, and for no good reason. In (8) the lines converge to form a solid, but the perimeter of that convergence edge is lumpy and uneven.

Interestingly, when designers reach too far, they can over-stylize or over-refine an identity to the point of making it unrecognizable. Prudential Life insurance (6) had this happen when they simplified their logo so much that people no longer perceived the Rock of Gibraltar. They had to back off to a stylized but identifiable graphic.

Likewise, the designers of the Ibsen wordmark took their quest for "leading edge" to such an extent that they hoped people would read a lower-case "l" from a mere dot (1). It is too much to expect.

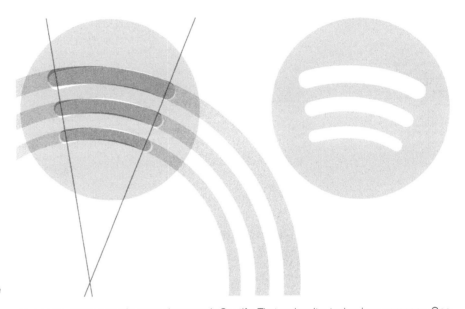

One of the leading music streaming apps is Spotify. That makes it a technology company. One might expect exactness in a logo for that kind of company. How sad that they have such an unrefined logo. One may look at the concentric arcs and think there's something a bit off. But when overlaid with geometrically drawn concentric arcs, one can really see what a slipshod job they have done with their logo. They've only been around since 2008 and have updated their identity two times since then, but never bothered fixing the sloppy arcs in their logo.

Deadly Sin of Logo Design #7:

Tiny Elements, Thin Lines

We have already dealt with the problem of overall mass. A similar but distinct issue is that of tiny elements or thin lines, even when found in a logo that has sufficient overall mass.

All kinds of printing, be it offset, digital, laser or ink jet, have a similar drawback. I call it Ink Creep: the ink from the bigger object fills in fine negative lines to some degree. If the lines are substantial enough, the line survives this minute encroachment. On the other hand, if the line is thin, it can be compromised or filled in. This is why experienced designers avoid printing type with small serifs in reverse: the serifs fill in. Fine reversed lines in a logo are subject to a similar fate.

Some of these were taken from magazines printed on glossy paper, with reproduction as good as one can expect, and yet, the logos have filled in. The fault is not in the printing but in the designs. Tiny lines also pose a problem when things are seen through a grid of pixels, as on the Web.

This problem is not eliminated in the digital world. We view all digital media through a grid of pixels. Admittedly, the grids are getting finer as screen resolutions for electronic devices go up. The resolution for the average computer screen, including the first two generations of iPads, now is 128 pixels per inch. While that is finer than the historical monitor norm of either 72 PPI (Mac) or 96 PPI (PC), it is not even double the resolution. Therefore, Pixel Mush reasserts itself. To review, Pixel Mush happens when shapes or lines are so small that they cannot be rendered with a pixel in the solid identity color or solid background color. If the identity colors are black and white, edges will be anti-aliased, which means that gray pixels are used on the edge to disguise the pixel grid. Anti-aliasing gives a smoother edge to elements on the screen and hides the "jaggies." But this useful technological help is a double-edged sword. In a black logo on a white background, very thin white lines may be rendered only in gray because the lines aren't wide enough for any pixels to be completely white or black.

This principle applies to typography as well, and is why fonts in the Didone family (such as Bodoni, Modern, Didot, etc.) are so seldom used in identity design. They have some nice, thick strokes, but they also have very thin strokes that tend to disappear.

Of all the Seven Deadly Sins, using is perhaps the most common error, second only to designing a logo that fails to work in black.

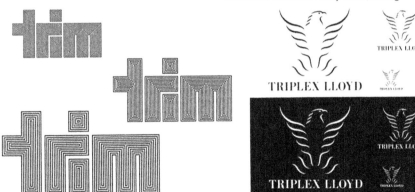

Sooner or later any identity will be used in reverse, so this principle applies to lines in any design that are either positive or negative. This is also why fonts with fine lines are problematic for identities; the fine lines tend to suffer in positive and fill in when in reverse.

elements too small or lines too thin

The "too small, too thin" sin is one of the few ever committed by great identity designers such as Paul Rand, Saul Bass and Chermayeff and Geismar. In virtually every case where they used tiny elements or thin lines, the identities have been replaced or amended. Over the years, countless designers for many companies have produced logos with lines that are too thin for good, solid reproduction. Most of these companies have redesigned their logos to correct this. Rand and Bass even corrected this mistake in their own logos, IBM and AT&T respectively. They have realized that you can't fight thin lines; you just have to get rid of them.

Some designers try to compensate by specifying that the identity ought not be used below a certain size. Unfortunately, many times identities must be used smaller than the "allowable" minimum. Companies routinely work with other companies where the identities of all participants will be shown in a "logo soup." The costs of newspaper ads and Yellow Pages ads often encourage the use of smaller identities. The coarse paper further aggravates the effects of tiny elements and thin lines.

Each of these identities had lines that were too fine and consequently did not reproduce at small or even reasonable sizes. In each case, the logos have been redesigned.
(Special note: Paul Rand recognized this problem in his first IBM logo and fixed it. Similarly, Saul Bass fixed this in his AT&T logo.)

Section 27

What's Left?

To recap the Seven Deadly Sins of Logo Design, they are:

B Can't work in **B**lack only
L **L**ack of mass
O **O**bscure contrast
W **W**ayward or disharmonious parts
O **O**verlapped elements
U **U**nrefined shapes
T **T**hin lines, **T**iny elements

It may not work for everyone, but an acronym like BLOWOUT helps me remember lists. I hope it works for you, too.

Some designers may be dismayed by this list and say, "If you take away all the approaches that cause a BLOWOUT, there's so little left. How can we work?"

Remember that the essential quality of any good identity is instant recognition and clarity. Anything that detracts from that is counterproductive and antithetical to what a good identity should be.

Others may be tempted to think, "All the good designs have been created using traditional methods. We have to go beyond them to find new and uncharted territory."

Still others may feel the old methods are too confining, too old-fashioned, too "been there, done that." They may think that for a truly contemporary identity,

J. S. Bach - Beginning of the Prelude from the Suite for Lute in G minor

one should use new visual techniques––even if they don't really work.

Let us compare our visual world to the world of music. In Western culture, the ancient Greeks worked out for us the diatonic scale of notes. From the simple octave with its twelve possible notes, no end of music has been composed, century after century, style after style. Notwithstanding the invention of new musical instruments, modern composers do not *require* new instruments to compose contemporary music.

If you were to hear on CNN, "Today the leading musicians of the world have agreed that no more good music can be composed; it's all been created," you might want to check to see if it's April Fool's Day.

All of the music that is possible from the same simple notes has not yet been written, nor will we ever reach a point where no new music can be created. In our analogy, new instruments could correspond to new visual media. How can we say, then, that our creativity as designers is being stifled by the need to use the same basic principles of visual clarity that have been honed and refined over the long history of identities?

Take heart. There will never be an end of good, well designed identities that work. Unfortunately, there will also be no end of poorly designed identities by people who have not learned the principles of the craft.

One need only look through design annuals to be inspired by new and marvelous design solutions for corporate identities. Sad to say, many of the bad examples shown in previous chapters were also published in these design annuals. Claiming that a design in a magazine is good doesn't make it so.

Remember: the purpose of a corporate identity is to clearly and instantly identify a company. Any factor that prevents that recognition is like the single hole in a balloon or a tire; it will cause a blowout.

But it is not enough to know what to avoid in the Seven Deadly Sins of Logo Design. This book is not just about what not to do; it is also about how to design the right way.

So If we go back to our exploration of the three identity components (wordmarks, logos and monograms), and we've had a good self-brainstorming session (or better yet, multiple sessions) to come up with some ideas with each of the four possible concepts (corporate activity, corporate ideals, corporate name and abstract), we still have to decide how we are going to model, render, draw our identity.

After Brainstorming

After using the conceptualizing techniques discussed previously, a designer will have a number of possible concepts for any given identity project. Naturally, many concepts will be rather raw. Even so, looking at the shapes made for each concept may provide some opportunities for cross-fertilizing ideas.

The shapes in one concept may be just what another concept needs to make it work. This may foster a new round of conceptualizing based on the first round. As mentioned before, this process is best done manually with pencil in hand, not on the computer. Go to the computer vector program only for the final rendering.

After this stage, it may be necessary to visually process one or more concepts. A number of techniques can transform elements into something unique and useful.

Does the way you work does the way you work
affect the way you think?
(the answer is yes!)

Visual Processing Techniques

Now let's look at some good visual approaches for executing a concept. Let's say you have decided on a lion as an appropriate concept for your client's logo. (Or an eagle, or a tree.) Any of those words may seem lame or over-used. Yes, there have been a million lion logos already, and maybe even half of them are good. That doesn't mean there can't be another good lion logo that is different from any lion logo that's ever been produced.

We've seen how you can kick-start your creative juices by pairing the three possible identity components with the four possible identity concepts. Similarly, you can develop a distinctive and esthetic mark through the main kinds of visual processing. I've identified ten of them. There may be more, and I'd love to hear from you if you know of another one.

To help with that process, I've developed another acronym: CPFULLNESS. It can stand for Creative Priming FULLNESS or Cool Potential FULLNESS, or maybe even ConcePt FULLNESS. (Yeah, I know that acronyms, by their very nature, can be a bit contrived. But they can be helpful, too.)

Next we'll examine some great examples of visual techniques.

Chapter Five

Core Principles

Visual
Techniques

Section 28

Visual Technique #1: Containment

I see Containment in two ways: Shallow Containment and Deep Containment.

Shallow Containment is merely placing a shape around a signature. Consequently, the image has not much more design value added than a plain signature. As I said before, a signature alone (merely choosing a certain font to write the company's name) is very little design value added and is mostly reserved for consumer product identities and the companies that make them. It is less well suited to other kinds of corporate identities.

Some uninspired designers will also add a shape to a poorly conceived or executed logo to mask its deficiencies. Again, Shallow Containment. It is an unfortunately common practice.

Shallow Containment: Placing a shape around a signature (mostly just selecting a font to write the company name). As with un-contained signatures, this technique is used mostly for consumer products and is not as suitable for other kinds of corporate identities.

On the other hand, the use of a containing shape can sometimes be the salvation of a decent design that might fail for other considerations, such as lack of contrast (16). In sample (1), for instance, the leading edge of a white golf ball would have no contrast against a white background. The addition of "zoom marks" on the dark side completes the edge. Containing a design can give it a logical boundary or stopping place for an image, like a picture frame (2, 8, 12, 23). Containers can contribute mass to designs that might be too insubstantial without them (2, 4, 6, 17, 20, 21). Containers can compensate somewhat for a color that is almost too light (14, 22), giving the design color mass, distinct from image mass already mentioned. Containers can provide unity and cohesiveness to word-cluster-style wordmarks or reinforce the shapes in a wordmark (7, 9, 13). Containment can echo the shape of a specific letterform (17, 18, 19, 22). Containers can contrast with the shapes contained (3, 5, 6, 12, 15, 20) or harmonize with them (7, 11, 14, 17, 18, 19). Containment can give symmetry or help center unsymmetrical shapes (3, 5, 8, 12, 14, 15, 20). Containment can change the overall shape of the significant design element ((3, 6, 10, 12, 15, 20, 22). Containment can be the template for the whole design (11, 19).

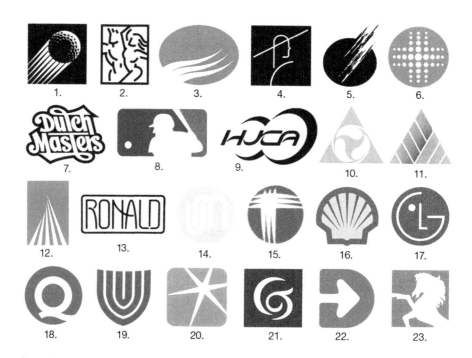

Containment is a useful visual treatment and should be part of every identity designer's tool box.

Section 29

Visual Technique #2: Planar or Silhouette

A planar image is one that renders shadows as a solid dark color, and lighter parts as a solid light color or white, with no shading (1-10). A silhouette is similar but uses only the contour of the whole subject and disregards any light falling on it (11-20).

Both of these are common techniques for making logos with strong imagery in solid colors. Most of the samples above are photographically realistic drawings; however, some (8, 10, 14, 20) use a non-realistic style.

Even though some of these designs use more than one color (3, 6, 7, 8 17, 18), the secondary colors could be printed in white or black.

A separate consideration from the overall drawing style (realistic or non-realistic) is the edge quality. This can add distinct flavor without changing the drawing style. Notice how the edges of each shape can be rectilinear -- all of (2), or just the face (6). On the other hand, all edges can be made curvilinear with

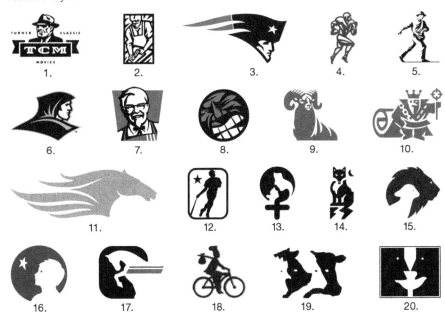

Top half: Logos using planar shapes to represent three-dimensional images while using solid colors.
Bottom half: Logos using silhouettes either as positive images or reversed out of a solid containment shape or another element.

either an s-curve or graceful arc (4, 11) and just the cloak (6).

Planar and silhouette renderings can also use other systems of shapes. For instance, (14) is an interesting combination of almost geometric curves with straight lines. The gold halo used on (18) can easily be omitted in one-color situations.

Here we can see the flavors of edge quality and its contribution to the end image. First we see a realistic rendering with natural edge quality. Second is a rectilinear rendering; notice that each shape is reproduced more or less accurately but only with straight edges. Next we see the same shapes with a curvilinear flavor; each edge is either an s-curve or a graceful arc. These edge quality flavors can be used on planar images as in this sample, or on silhouettes.

Section 30

Visual Technique #3: Fragmentation

A design can be broken up into smaller portions using stripes, dots, triangles or any other repeatable solid shape. These shapes can be tapered (in the case of lines) or rendered at different sizes (in the case of dots, triangles or squares). Grids can be employed to keep the units even or progressively larger and smaller. Vector programs like Adobe Illustrator can be useful in creating such fragmentations.

Fragmentation can give some of the benefits of gradients without the drawbacks. It can also give the illusion of different values while using one solid color, again, without any of its drawbacks.

When using fragmentation, avoid making any sub-shapes too small. Otherwise, you fall into the pit of Tiny Elements and Thin Lines (Deadly Sin of Logo Design #7). Rather than using twelve lines to fragment an element, try eight or seven. This is the very lesson that Paul Rand learned with his own IBM logo and Saul Bass with his AT&T logo (see Section 26).

When using tapering lines, it is important to avoid making the ends with too fine a tapering point. Such needle-like points can be subject to filling in or dropping off. Either make tapering lines with blunt tips or increase the angle of taper at the ends to make less visually fragile points. The value of doing this may not

As long as care has been taken to avoid Deadly Sin of Logo Design #7 (Tiny Elements or Thin Lines), fragmentation can be effective. A few of these could be improved with fewer parts.

be apparent with a positive version, but every logo ought to be able to be reversed. Printing any fragmented design in reverse may show fine points that are in danger of filling in.

When in doubt, try a test print of the logo design in positive, and reverse at only a half-inch high—or even smaller—on regular or even poor quality paper. Is the print clear? Do the fragmentations remain separate and clean? If not, try fewer fragmentations.

Recently there have been numerous logos designed that are made of many beautifully colorful facets. Some of them are breathtaking. But they are also fatally flawed because they typically do not reproduce well in grayscale, having poor internal contrast, and do not keep their faceted quality when rendered as solid black.

With some of these identities, the designers have seen the deficiencies and have designed an alternate design for one-color usage with separated facets. But this means that the one-color

version is actually a different design, which just underscores the original design's flaws.

The solution is simple. Just separate the facets into discrete parts with a gap between each element in the first place. This will prevent having a non-separated design and a separated design, which would be really two different designs. Here care must be taken so the gaps will not be too small but it will work in both the multi-color version and grayscale and in solid black.

A   B   C   D   E   F

Here are two samples of a common variety of very colorful logo being created lately (A). However, these often do not convert well to grayscale (B) and lose their multi-faceted quality altogether in one solid color (C). The solution is to fragment the facets to begin with (D). This may inspire an overall simplification, not a bad thing at all, but the result will hold together better as both grayscale (E) and in any solid color (F).

Visual Technique #4: Unique Coincidence

Every new client's corporate activity, ideals, name or initials carry unique visual opportunities that will work only for that particular kind of business and name or set of letters.

When conceptualizing, take some time to play with the letters or images involved. Imagine images upside down. Try them in mirror image. Look at the sketches you are considering. Are there shapes that can work well together? Explore different fonts and ways of making letters. Pay attention to overall shapes, to the negative spaces, to possible ways of joining shapes. Strip away preconceptions; let the edges blur in your mind. You are less likely to see unique coincidences at first glance when you are thinking too literally, or if you're working on a computer; they present themselves more often with paper and pencil.

These kinds of serendipitous joinings most often percolate to the top when you have time to fiddle with the bits and let the magic happen. Such coincidences can't be forced, but when they work well, they are a joy to see.

Classic Jazz

Dan Pearson Studio

Culture Bus

Atlantic Electric

City Direct

Studio Eight

TWINS
Twins

NEW MAN
New Man

BR baskin robbins
Baskin Robbins (31 Flavors)

Ryan Biggs

Sandra Berler Gallery

FontSmith

Henry Wilson

Reward
Reward

Eight
Eight

Dig

WebMonster

Hilton Construction

Peter Ryan

Zip

Hartford Whalers

Northwest Airlines

Art Machine

Texas Jet

Each of these concepts is unique to the particular letters used in combination with the corporate name, activity, ideals or fonts being experimented with. If that experimentation had not happened, these delightful identities would never have been created.

Visual Technique #5: Linear Treatment

As with fragmentation, the technique of rendering the whole identity with lines alone risks making the lines or spaces too delicate for clarity in small sizes or viewed from a distance. Drawing lines that are too lightweight for the overall size will make the whole logo too insubstantial (Deadly Sin of Logo Design #2: Lack of Mass). If lines are close together, it is safest to make lines and gaps the same thickness. Why? Gaps become positive lines when the identity is reversed.

The samples shown here have decent mass. When designing with this technique, a good test is to print a design at no bigger than one-half inch on plain paper. If it is indistinct or begins to blur or fill in, either the rendering needs to be simplified or the lines (or gaps between) need increased weight.

Mayfair News
by Ayce

Artica Fish
by Kabala Diseño

by Taylor Dolan

Valtur
by Studio Boggeri

Tomco Plastics
by John Noneman

CFO Cycling Team
by Logorado

by Ellen Lytle

Rehabilitation Hospitals of America
by John Langdon

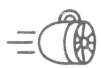
Turbean Coffee
by Focus Lab

by jonassoeder.de by jonassoeder.de

Despia
by Darkmatters

KMCC
by Mateusz Turbinski

Monarch Machinery
by Chris Yaneff

Generally speaking, fewer lines are better than many, and heavier lines are better than fine.

90

A good rule of thumb is: make all lines either of uniform thickness or of variable thickness. Don't mix techniques (remember: coincide or contrast). Tools like Adobe Illustrator are particularly good at keeping strokes exactly the same and separating one stroke from another at exact distances. Stroke caps and corners can be blunt, mitered or round.

We now can make vector strokes thicker or thinner. Here again, strive for the beauty and grace of simplicity. Bezier curved lines are inherently more graceful when the fewest possible anchor points are used. The same is true of making lines thick and thin: the fewest changes will give the most graceful lines. Even lines that just taper at the ends and are mostly of uniform thickness can be effective.

Another consideration is how lines join at corners. If they join with sharp points, that can accentuate the curvilinear quality of the line. Ironically, lines joined in rounded corners will just look blobby and not produce as curvaceous an effect.

Design Kitchen
by Dillan Powell

Electric Bird
by Yuri Kartashev

Ugly Dog Design

New York
Public Library

Flying Pig Logo

Mighty Dream
by Eric Grossnickle

Mazda

Wool

Visual Technique #6: Ligatures, Swashes and Flourishes

Ligatures and flourishes (or swashes) will be useful mostly as options for wordmarks and monograms because they are typographic in nature. Indeed, employing either can change a plain signature into a wordmark.

Ligatures

Typographic ligatures have existed from the first days when moveable type was invented, carrying over many of the handwriting conventions of the times into the new medium of printing. Letters in the words "The" and "And" were often combined into single ligatures, and dozens of other letter combinations were among the first sets of lead type ever cast. However, as many new sans serif fonts were not designed with ligature variants, the use of ligatures declined by the first half of the 20th century.

When I was a young graphic designer, I noticed the profound influence of the masthead for Herb Lubalin's new magazine, *Avant Garde*. Its radical typographic deviations inspired our generation to see typography less rigidly and more creatively. Lubalin designed a whole Avant Garde font with many new ligature variants so we could all explore ligatures.

A CA EA FA GA HT KA LA M NT RR RA ST TH UT V W

Some of Lubalin's ligatures in his Avant Garde font. Although ligatures were originally unique joinings of adjacent letters, the term now could apply to any alternative letterform variation.

Flourishes and Swashes

Another typographic variation that goes well with ligatures is the making of decorative additions such as swashes or flourishes.

Some of these typographic deviations can communicate either an antique or a modern quality. Flourishes and swashes can imply fun and recreation and are consequently popular in certain segments of identity design, such as the food and drink industry, restaurants and rock bands.

Ligatures can be old-fashioned or contemporary.

Credits: 1. Tom Nikosey, 2. Michael Manoogian, 3. Niels Shoe Meulman, 4. David Quay, 5. Jessica Hische, all others: unknown.

Again, the key rule is: do not impede legibility by obscuring letterforms. It is one thing to use convoluted type on a magazine article title, where it can be an entertaining puzzle. That doesn't work for wordmarks for corporate identities. The whole raison d'être of an identity is to be instantly and easily recognized. Designing a corporate identity that has to be deciphered, unraveled or decoded is not an option. You don't get three strikes; one strike and you're out. Sometimes designers get so fixated on typographic creativity that they don't realize that their decorations are conflicting with the letterforms, or that the design contains another visual conflict like poor contrast.

When used well, ligatures, swashes and flourishes are powerful tools that can contribute to memorable designs with strong and unique visual entertainment value.

The important rule here is to avoid letting decorations either upstage the core letterforms of words embellished (3, 6) or interfere with them (2). This is easier to accomplish if you keep the decoration(s) outside the core of the letterforms. Sometimes decent typographic designs are undone by unnecessarily complicating the design with offset strokes (1) or textured backgrounds (6). Sometimes a fine design is undermined by contrasting the drop shadow with the background, and not the actual letterforms, (4). Sometimes letterforms are so stylized that people have difficulty reading the message, a consideration separate from the swashes or flourishes used (5). The base letters are just too overwrought to be readable. The sad thing is that one doesn't have to sacrifice beauty for legibility (7, designed by David Ariail).

Swashes are most successful when the core letterforms are not compromised.

Section 34

Visual Technique #7: Negative Shapes

Most letters have negative shapes or counters. They are more malleable than the positive parts of letterforms and provide chances to create a double entendre while leaving the core letterform recognizable. Many other images also can have negative shapes, such as those you might develop using the four conceptual approaches (Chapter 3). Why not combine the techniques? See what the counters of the letters remind you of. Look at the elements you associate with the company activity, ideals or name. Those concepts, too, have negative shapes. You need to be open to a certain amount of visionary frolicking to let these ideas emerge (that's why you don't conceptualize on the computer). In the end, it doesn't matter whether you consider the result a Negative Shape or a Unique Coincidence (Visual Technique #4), as long as you find the potential magic.

Here is where broad exploration bears fruit from earlier self-brainstorming. This is also where you will see the value of not editing during your concept generation but rather, drawing all the concepts that come to mind. When you combine a negative shape with a solid shape, a concept that might have looked lightweight, trite or even cheesy at the early stages can turn into a stroke of genius.

Negative shapes allow a visual double entendre. It could look too contrived or forced if you work only with the positive shapes.

Visual Technique #8: Essence

In identity design the most important question to ask is not "What can I add to this design?" but rather, "What can I remove? How can I simplify it, stylize it?" and "How can I show the essence of this subject?"

As we have stressed before, a good logo is not an illustration or a photograph. It is a symbol that reminds us of something, but it needs to be elegant in its restraint. This has been the whole trend of the corporate-identity design industry for

the past century (see Section 10: A Brief Overview of Branding History, and Section 11: Evolution of High Profile Identities, as well as Section 12: Great Designers of the Last Century).

Simplicity is the soul of good design, and it is the key to identities that stand the test of time. Pare down, simplify and find the essence of the image. This is where you can make your design exquisite – before you add colors or any other bells and whistles. Make a solid

In the upper left is the old logo for Rockport Publishers and its newer replacement. See how the new, simpler logo is visually stronger, easier to read? Each other section shows logos not from the same company but using the same visual subject. In each case, the first samples are more literal on the left and simpler on the right. Notice how each of the simpler logos is stronger, can be seen and comprehended more easily and will be more memorable than the more detailed and literal versions.

foundation, and you can create great images on it. Skimp on this stage, and you will have made yet another mediocre logo that eventually will be replaced.

Of all the ten Visual Processing Techniques, striving for simplicity is one that should always be employed. Paradoxically, less detail can mean a clearer image.

Visual Technique #9: A System of Shapes

The term "system of shapes" may sound too formal and even a bit daunting to attempt, but it is just a way of saying that any design can contain simple, repeated elements.

Finding the subject for the logo is just the beginning. Even with the simplest concepts, such as a single-letter monogram, there is virtually no end to ways of drawing each letter or subject.

When using a system of shapes, one can impose a grid to reconstruct the image. Grids are handy for seeing relationships, measurements and angles. The grid can employ curved corners or not. Sometimes a particular curve or shape can be repeated to good effect. Those shapes could even come from the type font of the accompanying signature. Systems of shapes can be stylized, curvilinear, rectilinear, distorted, geometric or blended into some unique overall confining shape. The possibilities are endless, and surprisingly simple once you dissect them. As you begin

Making a unique mark from an ordinary letter or subject is not hard. Here we have some Ws, trees, lions, stars, hearts and hands, and owls. Each logo is different from others of the same subject because each was constructed with its own system of shapes. You could make a new tree by using the system of shapes from one of the lions. The possibilities are endless.

to look for them, you will see all sorts of different visual systems for making logos. It can be helpful to collect them for future reference.

One easy method for getting the hang of this technique is to look at an existing logo. To avoid plagiarism, don't use the same subject; just copy the style or system. Now construct your image using that style. *Voilà!* A new and unique design.

Here are 25 different eagle logo designs. Each uses repeated shapes, angles, line thicknesses. Some use geometric or other shapes to form parts. Each one is a system of shapes that could be used to draw a new logo. As long as the subject matter is different, you are not plagiarizing.

Almost any concept for a logo probably has already been used. It is the visual treatment that distinguishes various logos. That often involves using a system of shapes as well as combining elements. Within a given logo, don't use more than one system of shapes.

Visual Technique #10: Sculpted Type

Before the invention of moveable type, illustrated manuscripts featured hand-rendered lettering and embellished capitals. Hand typography was as free and as beautiful as its creators could make it. Although Gutenberg's invention for creating wordmarks with non-linear baselines that Gutenberg didn't have. With hand skills, even if digitally executed, one can produce excellent Sculpted Type for a wide variety of purposes, including identities.

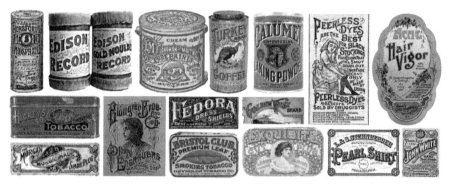

The beauty of what I call Sculpted Type (non-linear baselines), along with flourishes and swashes, is even more impressive when we consider that this typography was rendered by hand.

allowed more books to be printed, type was limited to flat baselines with letters all the same height. Early on, drop caps and embellished capitals were developed for printing, but the baselines remained flat. Over the years, the appetite returned for customized, or, as I like to call it, "Sculpted Type," with non-linear baselines and flourishes.

With the advent of the desktop computer, every designer has become a de facto typesetter, although with many of Gutenberg's original limitations. However, we now have digital tools

Both Photoshop and Illustrator (and their software counterparts) have "Type Warp" tools for doing this. Unfortunately, these "Type Warp" tools do not respect individual letters, being only mathematical algorithms processed on whole words. The best practitioners of Sculpted Type tend to not use these tools, and I strongly recommend against them also. Instead, designers can have much better results by changing individual letters with the "shear" tool and fine-tuning letters by moving vector anchor points individually.

Note that with the exception of the Splayed Arc, the verticals in each letter remain vertical. Text Warp tools don't do that well in some of these configurations.

Flourishes and swashes (Visual Processing Technique #6) are frequent, welcome additions to Sculpted Type. This approach can be particularly effective in wordmark design to evoke associations with either old-fashioned nostalgia or futuristic mystique.

Sculpted Type is popular with several sectors of identity design. For instance, music bands—especially in the heavy-metal genre—often use sculpted type for their identities. Unfortunately, it is surprising how often legibility will be sacrificed for the perceived "cool factor" effect. Illustrated here are mostly legible samples. Many more are nearly impossible to read. It almost seems as

Great examples of Sculpted Type: 2, 3 Martin Schmetzer, 5 Alan Ariail, 7, 8, 9 Tom Nikosey, 10 Dave Stevenson, 1, 4,11 unknown

Band identities do not have to sacrifice illegibility to be cool. Here are some decent examples, although the one in the lower right is more challenging to read. Credits: 5 Tom Nickosey, all others unknown.

though the designs are manifesting the nihilist sentiments these groups seem to both espouse and engender, and are almost daring the reader to understand the wordmark. If so, they are defeating a wordmark's very purpose.

Sculpted type is also popular in restaurant identities. Here, the association is with old-fashioned values, although sculpted type can also look contemporary. Either formality or informality can be communicated with this treatment. Sculpted type can be typographic fun.

Sculpted type is a favorite of the beverage industry, for both alcoholic and non-alcoholic products.

Restaurants are places of relaxation and good times. Sculpted type can add to that feeling and can look either old-fashioned or contemporary. Credits: 4 Scott Greci, 10 Alan Ariail, all others unknown

3. Ginger Monkey, 4. Andreas Grey, 6. Dave Stevenson, 7. Jason Thornton, 1, 2, 5 unknown.

The food industry is a heavy user of this technique. Many of type artists don't even start with existing fonts and most do not use Type Warp tools. Instead, product wordmarks are often hand-drawn, and highly customized even though ultimately rendered in vector.

Sculpted type probably is part of the subconscious of all of us. Many of us begin our days looking at sculpted type on the breakfast table without evening thinking about it.

Sculpted Type is here to stay. It's not what's needed for all wordmarks, but when it works, it is a remarkable technique.

Credits: 1-4 Alan Ariail, 5-17 unknown.

Credits: 1 & 6 Alan Ariail, all others unknown.

Working at Creativity

Can creativity be cultivated?

Albert Einstein is not remembered for his graphic design, but he was responsible for an abundance of creative new ideas—in the field of physics. Not all creativity is visual. Or musical. Or literary. Every area of human endeavor has the potential for creativity. Read what Einstein said: "As one grows older, one sees the impossibility of imposing your will on the chaos with brute force. But if you are patient, there may come that moment when, while eating an apple, the solution presents itself politely and says, 'Here I am!'"

To be sure, it is wonderful to have an inspired idea occur to you. It feels like magic. And if the idea really was inspired, it can work like magic, too.

How do those moments happen? I don't know. But I do know how to encourage them to happen more often.

One way is to get engaged, really, deeply invested in your creative project as *early* as you can. Puzzle over the issue. Be hard on yourself, and don't settle for a mediocre solution.

Then put the problem aside. Let your subconscious work on it for a while. Then come back to it and slave on it again. Then put it aside again or sleep on it. I can't tell you how often a beautiful solution has presented itself to me in a

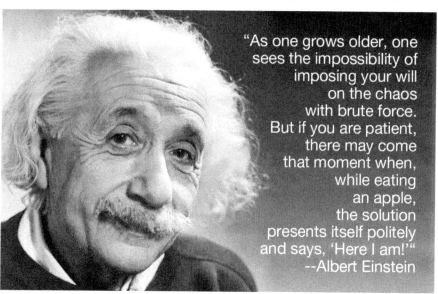

"As one grows older, one sees the impossibility of imposing your will on the chaos with brute force. But if you are patient, there may come that moment when, while eating an apple, the solution presents itself politely and says, 'Here I am!'"
--Albert Einstein

dream or when working on something completely different. The answer just percolates to the surface almost unbidden, as Einstein suggested. Most often, such inspirations really do work well.

But if you are a procrastinator, someone who gets to a job at the last possible moment, you can forget about "percolation time." To summon help, you have to get the subconscious truly engaged. Once that has been done, your subconscious will work on your issue while you turn your conscious attention to something else. The key is that you have to give your subconscious time. If you don't, it doesn't have a chance to come up with those breakthroughs.

You might think that Einstein was saying that you can't influence the process of getting inspiration, but if you know anything about how he worked, you will see that he was advocating the method I've just explained.

Here's another key principle: don't simply sit and wait for inspiration to strike. Leonardo da Vinci said: "It has long since come to my attention that people of accomplishment rarely sat back and let things happen to them. They went out and happened to things."

"It has long since come to my attention that people of accomplishment rarely sat back and let things happen to them. They went out and happened to things."
—Leonardo da Vinci

Why do I bring this up?

Because those who fail to be proactive are artistic dilettantes, dabblers, pretenders.

Chuck Close is a celebrated photographic-realist painter. He was born with prosopagnosia, a brain defect that leaves him unable to recognize faces. Paradoxically, he made a successful career painting giant, ultra-realistic portraits. In 1988, he suffered a spinal artery collapse that left him almost totally paralyzed. Most people would have given up painting at that point, but he did not. Since then, he has continued to create giant portraits. Because his finer motor skills have been ruined by the paralysis, he breaks his portraits into large, multicolored boxes, each presenting an overall color.

Chuck Close's triumph over such obstacles lends weight to his famous quote: "Inspiration is for amateurs — the rest of us just show up and get to work."

Some people imagine that creativity is a mystical phenomenon that can't be promoted or consciously influenced. I beg to differ (and apparently, so do Einstein, da Vinci and Chuck Close).

By your actions you can summon the muse. How do you increase the "eureka! moments"? One way is to stimulate as much of your brain as possible.

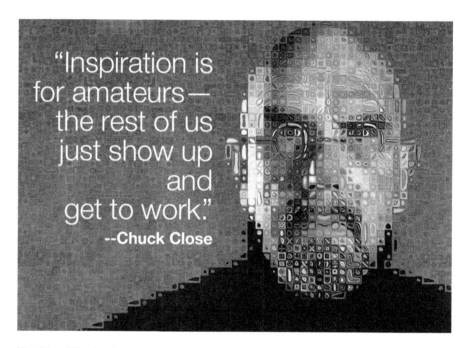

"Inspiration is for amateurs— the rest of us just show up and get to work."
--Chuck Close

Working The System

The system I have already explained does this. In relation to corporate identity design, we could make a checklist like this:

- Interview your clients.
- Discover specifically what they do
- Learn how they differ from their competitors
- Consider how their product or service might be represented simply
- Find out what their product or service does for their customers
- Discuss the ideals that they want associated with them
- Discover the association they most want to avoid
- Look up the meanings of their names (if any)

Sketch at least two concepts for each of the following combinations:

- Wordmarks showing corporate activity
- Monograms showing corporate activity
- Logos showing corporate activity
- Wordmarks with corporate ideals
- Monograms with corporate ideals
- Logos with corporate ideals
- Wordmarks showing the corporate name
- Monogram showing the corporate name
- Logos showing the corporate name
- Wordmarks using an abstract approach
- Monograms using an abstract approach
- Logos using an abstract approach

(This should give you a minimum of twenty-four concept sketches.)

Consider how each concept might be rendered with each of these visual processing techniques (even the weak, lame, stupid ones):

- Containment
- Planar or Silhouette
- Fragmentation
- Unique Coincidence
- Linear
- Ligatures and Flourishes
- Negative Shapes
- Essence
- System of Shapes
- Sculpted Type

Before executing any final designs, ensure that all seven deadly sins of logo design are avoided:

- Won't work in black only
- Lack of mass
- Obscure contrast
- Wayward or disharmonious parts
- Overlapping elements
- Unrefined shapes
- Tiny elements, thin lines

Can you even imagine that this process won't produce results superior to whatever haphazard method you could otherwise employ?

This method works.

But there's one catch:
YOU have to work at it.

No One Wants to be a Wannabe

Recently I was listening to a podcast in which a woman had given a lecture on book publicity (a subject on which she was an expert) to a group of self-publishers. After the lecture, a lawyer asked how he might get publicity for his book. The woman was taken aback, because that was precisely the subject of her whole lecture: pre-publication reviews, ongoing reviews in all the media, radio interviews, book distribution and so on. She tried to recap these principles for the lawyer, but he brushed her explanation aside and again asked the same question. Apparently the lawyer thought that, because he was established in his own profession, he somehow could jump the queue in the business of publishing.

To me, that's what a wannabe is: someone who thinks he or she can arrive at the top of the mountain without climbing it. The helicopter ride to the summit may work for rich ski bums on physical mountains, but not in the real world in any career. Wannabes are amateur dabblers who won't submit to the discipline of the art form, but still think they can make it as professionals.

Wannabes are different from hobbyists who are practicing an art for their own enjoyment. They are also different from beginners who are committed to learning their craft. Every proficient

designer was once a fledgling, even an "aspiring designer." There is no shame in that.

On the other hand, wannabes are guilty of the pride that makes them feel that they are special and are somehow exempt from the law of "paying your dues."

Equally absurd are those who think they have nothing to learn. I fully expect to learn many things from you, dear reader, by sharing this book. If I didn't, I'd assume I already knew it all. And I don't. But I have learned a few things, and I think others would like to learn them, too. Or at least consider them.

One of the differences between pursuing graphic design and working at a practical trade like plumbing is that we will never know it all. That, indeed, can be one of the joys of our profession—why it never gets old. So we are all learning, no matter at what stage we are in our career. And if we are legitimately always improving our craft, then we don't deserve the label of wannabe.

Chapter Six

Core Principles

Color,
Typographic
and Spatial Issues

Logo and Signature Color Basics

Every identity must be able to work in flat black and white (1). There are too many situations where this constraint is a reality to ignore it. Newspapers and the Yellow Pages don't do well with halftones, especially when the size is small. Businesses often print forms in black only, and some businesses have many forms. A solid black-and-white original will always reproduce better in photocopies and faxes.

Besides, as was mentioned in previous chapters, when color is allowed to dictate designs, it can be a distraction that allows esthetically inferior forms, proportions and shape refinements to slip by unnoticed, at least initially. Sooner or later shoddy work will be recognized for what it is.

Unless an identity is a wordmark, it will be made up of a monogram or logo and a signature. Both elements together, not the logo alone, make up the identity. Signatures should always get the greater contrast (2). This may seem counter-intuitive, because the logo typically takes much more time to design than the signature, but the rule remains valid. Why? Because the signature must be read. A logo is useful only if a viewer has seen it before and has learned its connection to a company. On the other hand, if the signature can be read, it has communicated, even for a first-time viewer. This is true with both positive

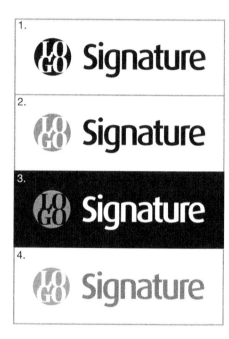

and reversed versions of an identity (3); the signature still receives the greater contrast. The vast majority of identities use a black signature. This might inspire the unwise to seek some other color for the signature "just to be different." Even in identities with a logo and a color signature, the signature should have no less than a 60% contrast with a background (4). A logo should have less contrast than a signature (a minimum of 40%) so that there is a natural hierarchy.

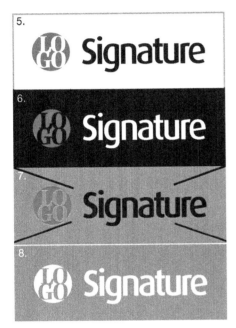

Color can be an important part of an identity, and every logo should be able to work in some color (5). When applying color, the signature still always gets the greater contrast, whether the identity is used positive or reversed (6).

But remember this inescapable fact: a color is also a value. A medium-red could be equivalent to a 50% gray, and might be used equally well as a positive or reverse identity (5, 6).

Since a signature needs at least 60% contrast, it is absolutely impossible to achieve that on a 50% gray. Also, a mid-value background will almost always kill the contrast with a logo (7). Therefore, mid-value backgrounds should be avoided wherever possible. When this is not possible, the only viable solution is to use an all-white identity (8).

If the color of a logo is darker than 60% in a positive identity (9), it will not work in reverse (10). One alternative is to use an all-white identity reversed out of the corporate color (11). But for true reversal versions, many companies employ an alternative color. It should not be just a tint of the original color (12) as the design will feel washed out. This is because white is totally neutral, and making a tint of a color will desaturate it. This will have a different emotional impact from the original color. An alternative reverse color version should keep the same degree of saturation, even if the hue is adjusted a bit to achieve an appropriately lighter value (13).

Advanced Color Issues for Identities

Color Contrast

An identity needs to work in all situations, not just in ideal lighting or at optimal distances. It must be easily recognizable in compromised lighting or less-than-ideal reproduction. What might look great on your computer monitor can (and most likely will) look different when printed. This is especially true with blues; they invariably print much darker than they appear on screen. Unless you print on the same machine every time, there will always be variance. Even printers of the same brand will vary considerably in color output.

This is why you can't cheat on, or be careless about, contrast as it appears on your monitor. The bare minimum contrast must be 40%. Why put your client's identity in jeopardy of being hard to read?

Identical digital files are shown here printed on three different machines of the same brand. Note how some elements have "good enough" contrast in one printing but very poor contrast in others. This is why designers cannot afford to trust their monitors or try to fudge contrast minimums. What good are identities that can't be seen and identified?

The contrast for a particular blue may look "good enough" on the screen, but blues almost always print darker than they show on screen. This identity was scanned from a glossy magazine print ad. Should a client be satisfied with an identity that doesn't show up?

Some think they are safe from color variations when designing for the web, but they're not. It used to be that you could design Web materials favoring the PC monitor gamma, safe in the knowledge that most viewers would see things as they were intended. Not any longer. Every year Apple sales (including iPhones and iPads) have increased to the point that a designer who favors only the PC monitor gamma setting will miss about half the market. Contrasts that look okay on one screen may not work on another.

For all these reasons, which should not surprise any professional designer, corporate identity design needs to include "contrast insurance." You absolutely cannot say that "close enough" will work, given all the variables of where an identity will be used.

As was mentioned in the previous chapter, a logo can have as little as a 40% difference with its background. But a color with only 40% contrast on white will have less contrast on a background such as pink or light blue – perhaps only 10% or 20%. Colors lighter than 40% will not provide enough contrast on white backgrounds and will be nearly invisible on other light backgrounds.

Colors darker than 80% are easily mistaken for black because of printing variances, so the client pays for color but does not get the benefit.

Reversals on black should also follow the same 40% guideline. Very few colors

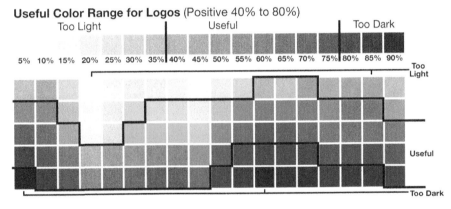

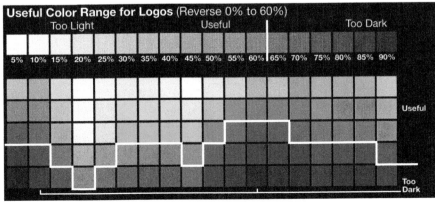

will work reasonably for both positive and reverse situations. Even so, if the background isn't black, but a dark color, the 40% difference should still be maintained.

The most common practice in identity design is to use color for the logo and black for the signature. If two different colors are used, it is important to remember these two principles:

1. The signature gets the greater contrast.

2. There should be a noticeable difference in value between the two colors.

If a value difference of about 40% is used, the widest range of color combinations is possible. In these cases, the lighter color needs to be in the range of 40% to 50%, and the darker color in the range of 60% to 80%. When a non-corporate color is used, the convention is to reverse an identity in white out of any dark-enough non-corporate color.

No color identity will work on every value of background. Logo colors at about 50% value may work equally well in positive and reverse, but only if the backgrounds are white or 10% or, alternatively, black or 90% respectively. As a result, many companies will have one corporate color that is used for

The whole identity in black only

The whole identity in the corporate color; must be at least a 60% value to give signature contrast.

Color logo and black signature

Two color identity, must be noticeable value difference; logo 40%-50%, signature 60%-80%

Reversed out of the corporate color; best if it is at least 60% value

Lighter color reversed out of the darker color, signature in white

Black and white reversed

Lighter color logo reversed out of black with white signature

Whole identity in lighter color reversed out of black

Whole identity in white on any dark enough non-corporate color

white and light backgrounds, and a similar but lighter alternative for reversals.

Designers who use an inappropriate color, like a bright, pure yellow, because of some association with the product will find that it just doesn't work on white backgrounds. This is one reason that primary colors never work.

In the chart shown here, the corporate color is used for the logo alone and black for the signature (top of left column). The result will be a range of compatible backgrounds that will give the 40% contrast needed.

If the corporate color is at least a 60% value, it may be used for both logo and signature (top, center columns), but even with an 80% value, only a narrow range of backgrounds will give the minimum 60% contrast needed for the signature.

Generally speaking, mid-value backgrounds should be avoided. It can be impossible to obtain enough contrast between such a background and any corporate color. When mid-value backgrounds cannot be avoided, often only an all-white version of the identity will give enough contrast (right column).

Many identities that use a darker color will require another corporate color for reversals. In the bottom of the left and center columns, the "Alternate Questor

Signage Films

AVERY

A5 New Translucent Colors
(For Backlit Signs)

Aqua" is used, but with the same contrast constraints: 40% for the logo, 60% for the signature.

Signage and Vehicles
Most businesses need signage or vehicles identified. Since most signage and vehicle graphics are done in vinyl, it is a wise precaution to pick an identity color from one that is already available in vinyl. Not every color in the Pantone book comes in a matching vinyl, but you

can get a matching Pantone ink for every standard vinyl color that exists. It makes sense, therefore, to look at vinyl colors before committing to any corporate identity color.

Custom vinyl colors can be made, but the client has to order thousands of rolls of such a color. While this may be fine for a national company, it is out of the question for a medium or small firm. Yes, one can get full-color printed vinyl now, but again, the cost is more than the standard-cut vinyl, and process-printed vinyl isn't as colorfast and doesn't last as long as solid vinyl. For companies with large fleets of vehicles, this is not a small financial consideration.

After choosing a vinyl color, it is a simple matter to identify the equivalents in Pantone inks, CMYK, RGB and Hexidecimal. This will enable corporate identity to be as consistent as possible across different media.

Internal Contrast

Another factor that too many designers fail to consider is internal contrast. Here again, a 40% minimum contrast is needed between touching elements. If you use black for containing shapes, for instance, colors used for fill need to be 60% or lighter to provide the minimum internal contrast of 40%.

Questor Aqua
Pantone 322
CMYK:
C100, M0, Y33, K35
RGB:
R0, G123, B133
Hexidecimal:
007b85
Vinyl:
Avery Nautical Blue
A8650-O

Questor Reverse Aqua
Pantone 7467
CMYK:
C95, M0, Y25, K0
RGB:
R0 G174 B197
Hexidecimal:
00aec5

This identity is legible in black. In the color-filled version, the colors are too dark to give sufficient internal contrast. The red is marginal at best, and the blue is way too dark to be easily distinguished from the black. This can be corrected with colors lighter than a 60% value, which will gives the 40% minimum difference needed with the black containing shapes.

(left) This logo was featured in a design annual as an innovative design. It isn't. Not only does it not reproduce in black only, it also has internal contrast problems. And besides all that, it needs three shades of olive green, two of which are not available in solid vinyl.

Remember, a professional works in the client's best interests, and any decision that will incur such an added expense should be the client's decision, not the designer's.

Busy Backgrounds

Boston Pizza recently redid its identity. It was not an improvement. It would have been far better for the circle containing the monogram BP to have been plain white. The new logo has a built-in busy background, which makes it very hard to read at a distance where properly designed logos are quite readable.

Beyond that, the brown building background is close in value to the red signature, making it vanish. Altogether, very difficult to see and a massive expenditure for that company to end up with a worse identity than before.

Difficulties with Reversals

Most logos can be used in reverse without any problem. However, if the logo imagery is using values to indicate three-dimensional solid with highlights and shadows, a reversal will not give the desired effect. Another difficulty happens when part of the logo represents something that must be light; switching that element to dark in the reversed version will, again, not give the desired effect.

The former AT&T logo could not be used as a straight reversal because it would have looked like the Death Star from Star Wars. Instead, a unique variation was designed for use in reversal situations that avoided this appearance. The KFC logo if reversed looked like an X-ray; they had to use a positive face over the reversal background. The lighthouse below looks like it broadcasted darkness in a true reverse. Here also, an alternate positive logo was inserted into the reversal background.

Original Positive Logos

Accurate but Inappropriate Reversals

Adjusted Reversal Versions

Typographic Issues with Signatures

nutella Neutrogena® **Pentel.** COVERGIRL®
Míele **PENTAX** **Nikon.** marie claire
TOSHIBA cacharel **ILFORD** **DIESEL**
Canon® **maxell.** NOKIA **TAMPAX**®

Trends in Signatures

For our purposes, we've defined a signature as the company name written in a particular font, with minimal or no design adjustments. As was said before, this is the least value-added design and has been used historically mostly for identities of consumer products. Signatures are not as suitable for other kinds of identities.

Interestingly, in recent years some companies, even in the consumer product arena, have redesigned their identities to be more than just a signature, or to add a logo to their existing signatures. Apparently they have found that a signature wasn't enough by itself. Beyond that, many consumer brands are using custom hand-rendered wordmarks (like the Barbie signature shown here) instead of merely employing a particular font.

Having said all of that, it is still the normal practice to have a signature

mazda
HERSHEY'S
Lipton.
OLYMPUS
BASF
Jeep.
GUCCI
Knorr
Barbie

These companies used to have plain typographic signatures but have redesigned them by adding another graphic element or adding a proper logo.

accompany a logo or a monogram. In that case, the signature follows our original definition: the company's functional name printed in a particular font. So even if a signature alone will not suffice, it is still part of identities except for wordmarks (and even most of those start out as signatures before the integration of unique design elements).

Trendy vs. Timeless

Many designers will want to use a distinctive font in a signature. It's natural that we don't want our signature to look like so many others. But that's not what we see in the best identities. Why? Because you don't want your signature type to look passé in a few years. So if you use the latest "in" font, chances are it will look tired in a few years. Many companies have learned this the hard way. We should learn it the easy way, by benefiting from their experience.

Remember, the more personality a font has, the more likely it is to become dated and look tired. Many companies that used the more idiosyncratic fonts have had to redesign their identities to look contemporary. Unfortunately, looking contemporary is what led them to that problem in the first place. What is needed instead is to look timeless.

Ask yourself, "Will this font stand the test of time?" That is what a good signature should do.

Each of these signatures has been redesigned to use type that will look less dated in a few years. Not all of them have succeeded.

Legibility Above All

Some designers think it's leading edge to be ultra-modern or even cryptic. It is just bleeding edge, not leading edge— rather like gluing thumbtacks point-up on a saddle, thinking they will keep the rider from falling off. For the public, the effort to decipher these signatures may not be worth the bother.

The absolute first requirement of a signature font is clarity. One might conceive of a seesaw with clarity on one end and personality on the other. If personality goes up, clarity most often goes down. Scripts, for instance, are among the least easy font groups to read instantly. There is a reason why we see so few "fancy" fonts used in identity design. Typically, the fancier the font, the lower the readability.

Another reason to opt for type with less personality is that you don't want the signature vying with the logo or monogram for attention. The logo should attract and entertain the eye, while the signature identifies whose logo it is. If the signature has too much personality, there will be a tug-of-war for the viewer's attention.

What were these designers thinking? Did they imagine that people wanted to play a guessing game? The last two samples on the right are not totally illegible, but neither has their treatment promoted instant readability, which should be the goal.

Signature Weight

Since clarity is essential if an identity is to do its most basic job, there are real drawbacks to a signature with no mass (see Deadly Sin of Logo Design #2: Lack of Mass). When signatures with no mass are used in a small space, the signature's legibility will fade. Even worse, when (not if) an identity is used in reverse, the signature's letterforms will fill in, no matter what kind of printing is used. While signage in cut vinyl will not fill in when reversed, signage is usually viewed at a distance, which will have the same visual effect.

This issue does not go away on the Web. Because there are only 72 pixels per inch (nominally) on the Web, very fine strokes don't show up as solid black (or white when reversed). This can mean that none of the pixels of a uniform-stroke typeface (as in Dax Light) or a thick-and-thin-stroke typeface (as in Bodoni) will show up as black or white respectively.

(right) Signatures are easier to read at a distance or at small sizes if the type has some mass. Fonts that have thick and very thin strokes also suffer especially when printed in reverse. This problem does not go away on the web, where thin strokes are so small that the pixels making them are neither the pure foreground or background color.

Signature
Signature
Signature
Signature
Signature
Signature
Signature
Signature

Signature **Signature**
Signature Signature
Signature Signature
Signature Signature

Signature **Signature**
Signature Signature
Signature Signature
Signature Signature

123

Kerning

Even though a signature with a logo or monogram is just type set in a particular font, you can't use it without perfect kerning. Kerning means adjusting the spaces between letters so that they appear uniform. While this is not done for body copy text, it becomes extremely important in identity signatures. These words will be seen at all different sizes and over a long time, and spacing can become quite noticeable, even irksome, if proper kerning is not done.

One simple way to discover where kerning is most needed is to look at words upside-down. Even better, look at them upside-down and backwards, perhaps through a piece of paper. Instead of noticing the letters, you then should notice any uneven spaces between them. To achieve good kerning, it is often acceptable to let two letters touch. Indeed, many signatures have tight letter spacing to begin with, so that all or most of the letters touch anyway.

If you are inexperienced at kerning, you can try printing your proposed signature in larger and very small sizes. Notice whether there are any kerning issues.

Much will depend on the particular letter combinations. Capital Ws and Ts, for instance, may have other letters nestling under their overhanging parts. Capital Ls naturally make a large void on the

Proper Type Kerning

ɓuᴉuɹǝʞ ǝdʎꓕ ɹǝdoɹԀ

Proper Type Kerning

The key to proper kerning is to equalize the negative spaces between letters. Viewing a line of type upside down makes it easier to see problem areas. Identity typography must have excellent kerning.

Examples of poor kerning are all about us. Sometimes over-kerning can be a problem, as seen in the two samples in the lower right. Here the better solution to the problem of capital L's could have been easily solved by using upper and lower case instead of all caps.

right and are prime candidates for joined ligatures with the next letter (see Visual Technique #6: Ligatures, Swashes and Flourishes). The possible combinations and needs for kerning are as varied as the words in our language.

Signatures and Extra Letter-spacing

It has become trendy to add extra letter-spacing to signatures (called tracking in most graphics software). Generally speaking, this is a counter productive design decision, for two reasons:

1. Extra letter-spacing makes a word read less naturally; visually speaking, the words don't hold together as well.

2. Extra letter-spacing makes the signature type smaller in the same space than it would have been with normal or even tight tracking.

Graphic design always has space limitations: page size, ad widths, column widths, and so on. To ignore this fact of our profession is absurd. It is equally unrealistic to think that size doesn't matter, at least as far as legibility is concerned. If signature type is smaller than it needs to be, it will, therefore, become illegible sooner than a signature with normal tracking.

The length of a signature has a direct bearing on the danger of extra letter-spacing. As you can see, more tracking merely weakens a medium-size signature but can be disastrous for long signatures. In the end, only short signatures survive this treatment, (there are many in use now), but that doesn't mean it improves readability.

Letterspacing

Letterspacing

Letterspacing

Letterspacing
Letterspacing
Letterspacing

Letterspacing
Letterspacing
Letterspacing
Letterspacing
Letterspacing

Type with extra tracking will be much shorter in the same horizontal space compared to normal letter-spacing.

Short
Medium
Lengthened
Short
Medium
Lengthened

Short
Medium
Lengthened

Extra tracking is more harmful to longer signatures than to shorter ones

125

Extended, Regular or Condensed Type?

A separate but related issue is type width. Any font is inherently condensed (1), regular (2) or extended (3) in its overall aspect. By their nature, shorter signatures have the flexibility to use fonts of any aspect. Medium-length signatures are less flexible, but successful signatures are possible with all three. As we have already established, when a signature is wider than it needs to be, it will also be shorter, and therefore, harder to read. Therefore, long signatures benefit most from condensed fonts and benefit least from extended fonts.

Short[1] [2]**Short** [3]**Short**
Medium **Medium** **Medium**
Lengthened **Lengthened** **Lengthened**

All Caps vs. Upper and Lower Case

Many studies have been done on the relative legibility of all capital letters versus upper and lower case. These studies measured instant recognition of words on highway billboards, where a viewer might be able to spare a mere second or less to look while driving. The studies showed that words in upper and lower case were easier to read than those in all caps.

Does this have implications for identity design?

Given that instant recognition is a fundamental goal of any identity design, it may. Consider also that some difficult kerning issues (L followed by A, W followed by Y, etc.) are lessened or not an issue at all in lower case.

What about using all lower case?

In our Western culture we capitalize first letters of proper names, and a signature is definitely the proper name of a company, so the first inclination would be to use upper case for the first letter. Too often, new designers choose all lower case "just to be different." As we have discussed earlier, that is an immature reason if it doesn't make the design stronger.

Besides that, using all lower-case letters can make a name seem less worthy of respect. That is not to say that all lower-case signatures should never be done, but they should be done for esthetic reasons, not in an attempt to be trendy or avant garde.

Does this mean that all caps are unsuitable for signature design? No. Many fine and successful signatures are in all caps. But it does mean that if a given word poses difficulties, a designer should always consider upper and lower case.

Section 42

Spatial Issues with Identities

Much of the good in a design, even in an exquisite design, can be undermined by poor spacing. There is no benefit to having size relationships that are jarring or spaces between elements that do not look natural.

Visual logic is one way to accomplish this. That is simply that shapes and sizes that are repeated make visual sense to our eyes. They seem natural, expected, right.

Gaps or spaces between elements of an identity that are based on visual logic don't call attention to themselves. After all, if the spaces drew one's attention instead of the elements, that would be counter productive design.

Logo vs. Signature Sizes

Logos and Monograms usually require an accompanying signature. A logo and signature together constitute the identity. (A notable exception is Apple. Only when your company is as big as Apple, can you omit the signature.) Logos and signatures shouldn't fight each other. The beginning designer will naturally care more about the logo than the signature because that was the part that usually was worked on more compared with the signature. Some want to display the logo big and the signature small, but this is a mistake. There should be a harmony between logo and signature. Size relationships should be balanced.

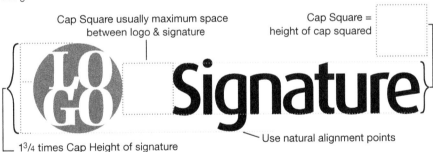

Cap Square usually maximum space between logo & signature

Cap Square = height of cap squared

Use natural alignment points

1³⁄₄ times Cap Height of signature is a good rule of thumb maximum logo size when at the side

Half Cap Square minimum space between logo and signature

1¼ times Cap Height of signature is a good rule of thumb minimum logo size when at the side

When a logo is at the side of the signature it will generally look balanced if it is between 1¹/₄ to 1³/₄ times the signature cap height. If it is smaller than that, it will appear insignificant. If the logo is much bigger than 1³/₄ times the signature height, it will appear to be eating the signature like PacMan gobbling its food.

Another factor is the amount of space between the logo and the signature. If the logo is too close, it will interfere with the instant reading of the signature, weakening the identity's effectiveness. If it is too far away, they will not feel connected. Another good rule of thumb for this space is between one cap height and a half cap height distance between them.

When the logo is above the signature in a vertical format, the identity will usually look balanced when the logo is 1¹/₂ to 2 times the cap height of the signature. A common vertical space between the logo and the signature is the x-height of the signature, measured from either the signature x-height or the cap height.

Other factors can influence what will look balanced including the size and weight of the signature. The number of words in the signature may also make a big difference. A two word signature would need a larger logo when the signature words are stacked flush left with the logo at the side. If the signature is all caps it may need a proportionately

When Logo is above:
Logo up to 2 times
Cap Height of
signature
(sometimes more
with a larger signature)

Minimum vertical space
is x-height of signature
May measure from
cap height or x-height

Cap
Height

Signature

x-height

Minimum size
1¹/₂ times
cap height
of signature

Minimum space
x-height of signature
May measure from
cap height or x-height

Cap
Height

Signature

x-height

larger logo to balance. Still, the above rules of thumb are good starting places.

128

Clear Space

Every identity needs a certain amount of space that belongs to it alone. Nothing else may come into this Clear Space, not even the company's own return address on stationery, for instance. Clear space is measured from the outside of the perimeter of any parts of an identity. Individual signature descenders are sometimes excluded from this perimeter calculation or they may be included, as in the samples shown here. The Clear Space should never be less than the x-height of the signature. Many times, it is the cap height of the signature, occasionally, even more.

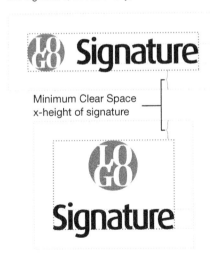

Minimum Clear Space
x-height of signature

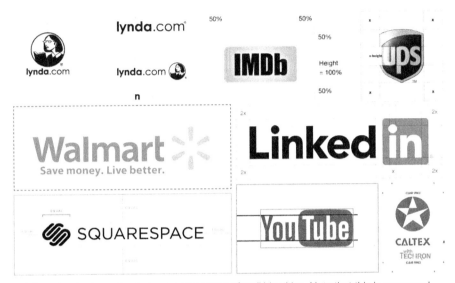

It is a standard practice to have a clear space for all identities. Note that this is measured from the outer edge of the whole identity, not just the logo. Some companies shown here did not give their identities enough clear space. This will result in crowding the identity in various design situations, a visual disrespect to the identity. Recommended absolute minimum clear space is the signature's x-height.

Notice that measurements for clear space— as well as all other spatial measurements— have been made *not* using inches, points, or millimeters. All measurements have been internal to the identity, such as the signature's x-height or cap height. Not only does this make all measurements automatically scalable, but it also is a natural way to achieve visual logic.

Slogan or Corporate Activity Phrase

Many well-known companies have slogans that they incorporate into alternate variations of their corporate identity. These slogans tend to change over time according to new marketing directions. Some examples are:

McDonald's	I'm lovin' it
FedEx	When there is no tomorrow
IBM	Solutions for a smart planet
Coca-Cola	Open Happiness
Nike	Just do it
KFC	Finger lickin' good

But slogans are not for everyone; they only work for companies that are so well-known that they don't need to tell people what they do or companies whose name is so descriptive that there is no need to explain further. All other companies should not use a slogan; what they need is a Corporate Activity Phrase (CA Phrase for short), some brief word or words that explains what they do.

When I was a teen I saw trucks driving around with the name Purolator on them (and nothing else). What's a Purolator? I thought maybe they made machines that made really good tasting coffee by filtering it (percolator / pure-olator?). Apparently I wasn't the only one who didn't know who they were or what they did because a few years later, they began to include the single word "courier" on their truck identities. That's a corporate activity phrase (or CA Phrase).

A business named Murphy's could be a men's clothier, a restaurant or a funeral home. Without a corporate activity phrase included with their identity, much of their advertising, especially that on vehicles or other out-of-context situations is largely wasted. If I don't already know what Murphy's does, I still won't without a corporate activity phrase. The key is that they be simple and clear. Examples might include:

Tax Consultants
Industrial Robotics
Pharmaceuticals
Natural Foods
Divorce Lawyers
Hydrogen Fueled Engines

For any businesses like these—and a million other ones not as famous as FedEx—a CA Phrase (not a slogan) should be incorporated into the identity for use whenever it is out of context or when a viewer might not already know what the company does. It goes on business cards, but perhaps not on the letterhead (because the letter can explain that better, if needed). It goes on signage and vehicle graphics. It goes on ads and brochures.

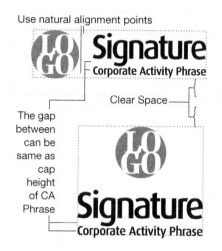

When a corporate activity phrase is used, it is considered part of the identity. The best place for it is under and smaller than the signature. It should be in the same color as the signature to not draw undo attention to itself. The ideal spacing is to have a gap between it and the signature equal to the corporate activity phrase's own cap height. That spacing always works, depending on the existence and depth of any signature descenders and on the length and height of the activity phrase. And it's visual logic.

Logo Aspect

Wordmarks tend to be much wider than they are tall. And there are successful logos of just about any shape: tall, wide, irregular, etc. Even so, there is a natural advantage to having a logo with close to equal height and width. Squares and circles, for instance, are more versatile than shapes much more extreme in aspect. That doesn't mean they can't be used; it just means they are less versatile in different design layout situations.

When these principles of visual logic are practiced with care, there is an increased esthetic added to any identity design.

One of the advantages of having a logo separate from a signature is that there can be different arrangements. Logos with the same vertical and horizontal dimensions (or close to it) are inherently easier to work along with a signature than a logo of extreme aspect.

Famous Fails

If I don't know about the law of gravity and I trip, I will still fall. It never fails. Ignorance of immutable laws gives no immunity to the outcome of breaking them. An infant who does not comprehend that fire is hot will get burned as badly as an adult who knows better.

Some may think my Seven Deadly Sins of Logo Design are just my arbitrary opinions, and as such may be either accepted or easily discounted. The whole purpose of this book has been to let you see with your own eyes that violating these principles can break an identity. You can run, but you can't hide from unalterable, immutable principles. It doesn't matter whether you are a famous designer or a beginner; if your identity is guilty of one of the Deadly Sins of Logo Design, it won't work, at least not consistently.

Here are three examples of large, world-class corporations that have changed their identities to new designs – which do not work.

AT&T

The excellent AT&T identity designed by Saul Bass was changed in 2005 after a corporate restructuring. The new design is an homage to the Bass logo, but it is a weaker version. As with so many designs that start from the color 3-D version instead of a plain, solid form, the shapes are less than esthetically refined. The design doesn't do well printed in a single flat color, which means that ALL printing for this company must be in full color. This is particularly noteworthy when vehicles and signage are considered. Instead of the more durable cut vinyl in solid colors, ALL vehicles and signage must be done in printed vinyl. It looks cool, but it tends to fade sooner, meaning quicker replacement times. This is a massive extra expense for a company that has so many thousands of vehicles. Besides, the darkest parts of the new logo are barely a 40% value (minimal contrast), and most are much lighter, giving the overall logo poor contrast.

Deadly Sins of Logo Design committed in this new identity:
  • Does not work in just black.
  • Unrefined shapes
  • Poor contrast

Sounds like three strikes and you're out.

The progression of the AT&T identity with the Saul Bass logo in 1993, which was improved by him again in 1996. Then they adopted an inferior logo in 2005.

When you render the new AT&T logo stripes in black you see the wonky nature of some of those shapes. On vehicles and signage, the logo can not be made of solid material and has minimal contrast. Recently, AT&T has recognized the contrast issues of their logo and have even tried to address some of the unrefined shapes. Note that this slightly improved variation only works in reverse and still does not have a positive version.

United Airlines

Saul Bass also designed logos for United Airlines and Continental Airlines. They were classic logos that could have lasted forever, but both were replaced after Continental bought United. Both airlines traded two superior logos for one inferior one. The new Continental/ United logo commits the deadly sin of too-small elements and lines. As a result, they don't reproduce well in a myriad of applications. The fine lines in the logo get deformed when printed on the company's own boarding passes. How many thousands of passes are given to customers every day?

I flew on Continental last year. The flight was OK. The seats had individual movie screens on the back for watching in-flight movies. Nice. But on start-up, for quite a while before the airline had any movies, they only showed the Continental identity. The screen was good enough for movies, but the logo's lines were so small there just weren't enough pixels for each line to be either white or blue. It looked horrible. Pixel mush.

Continental paid a pretty penny to have its new logo designed, you can be sure. But that is just a drop in the bucket compared with the cost of implementing the new identity. When you consider the size of the graphics that go on airplanes alone, the cost to put the identity on

The Continental identity as it appears on the screens of the company's own plane seats. The logo parts are too small for individual pixels to be the correct blue or white.

every plane is staggering. And how many planes do the two combined airlines own? In addition, there are other vehicles, signage, and so much more. What a monstrous expenditure to implement a broken logo.

Deadly Sin of Logo Design committed in this new identity:

- Lines too thin, elements too small

Xerox

When you think Xerox, you likely think copiers, right? Now the company has graduated to earning the bulk of its revenue in higher end printers. It is particularly paradoxical then to see this latest identity from Xerox.

It doesn't print well.

A

B

C

Xerox paper comes in nice white cartons labelled with the new Xerox identity. Most printing on cardboard is done with Flexography. This amounts to a giant rubber stamp mounted on a drum. Look at the fine lines that crisscross in the middle of the logo (A). See how deformed they are? Why? Because those lines were printed from a raised rubber printing plate.

1906

1949

1954

1954

1957

XEROX
CORPORATION
1961

XEROX
1968

XEROX
1968

THE DOCUMENT COMPANY
XEROX
1994

THE DOCUMENT COMPANY
XEROX.
2002

XEROX®
2004

xerox
2007

Inside each carton are several reams of printing paper, each with a printed wrapper. The wrappers appear to be printed in letterpress so that the plates can hold up to the millions of wrappers printed. The logos are black and red (B). In addition to the black being slightly out of register with the red, the lines are blotchy. And this logo is not on crude cardboard as on the box, but on fine, semi-gloss paper. Still the printing is poor.

Lastly, when you go to use a Xerox printer, the machine has a color touchscreen. But even here the logo cannot reproduce well (C). The crisscross lines in the middle are a light gray that gets lighter in the reflected light on the logo's spherical surface. The lines look totally bleached out.

How ironic to have a company whose bread and butter is printing reproduction with a logo that reproduces so poorly. Isn't that the definition of abject failure for whoever was involved in that identity design?

Deadly Sins of Logo Design committed in this new identity:
- Multiple colors in the logo
- Thin lines, tiny elements
- Poor contrast

Just these three examples represent
hundreds of thousands, perhaps
millions, of dollars wasted on inferior
graphic design and the implementation
of those designs. The saddest thing is
that there is no need for weak identities
like this in the first place. The principles
we've spoken of here are bedrock and
immutable. They do not move aside for
fad or fashion. They remain true whether
you believe in them or not.

The good news is that these principles
can be learned by anyone with the
clarity of thought to recognize them and
the discipline to practice them.

Superior design awaits.

Section 44

Responsive Logos, Avatars and Favicons

Responsive Logos

Many of us now do a significant amount of web surfing on tablets and smart phones, not just our desktop or laptop computers. Hence the rising use of responsive websites, sites that change the size and organization of a page's content, depending on the device used for viewing it.

Because of that, many companies also have what are now being called "responsive logos" which means that they change to suit the web device screen size they are being viewed on. When we see how effective the pared down versions are, it makes you wonder: with the exception of the last versions without a signature, why didn't the designer do that in the first place? Then there wouldn't need to be this alteration for different screen sizes.

Each of these companies has four increasingly simpler responsive logo variations.
Images courtesy responsivelogos.co.uk

137

Social Media Avatars

One would have to be living on another planet to not know how important social media is, not just for individual people today, but for all sorts of companies as well. Facebook, Twitter, Pinterest and Instagram are the most popular but the list goes on.

Social media allow the user to have an avatar, a visual portrait of the person—or for companies, their logo. An avatar can be nice and big on your own page in these sites, but the avatars on your notices, tweets or posts going to followers are quite small. As of this writing, here are the typical sizes of avatars for the big four social media and their avatar sizes for posts or tweets:

Twitter	42 pixels square
Pinterest	40 pixels square
FaceBook	32 pixels square
Instagram	30 pixels round

Obviously, clear and simple logos survive best in this social media arena. Logos without any of the Seven Deadly Sins do better than faces with such a limited number of pixels.

Instagram avatars as they appear on iPhone posts. Unfortunately, some seem not designed for this size but for larger profile page avatars.

Favicons

We'll end our journey with the humble little favicon (*fav* rhymes with *have*), short for favorite icon. These tiny nuggets of branding design can (and should) be part of every commercial website. When we visit any website that has a favicon, it will appear at the top of the browser window or tab. If we have multiple tabs in use in our browser, the favicon appears in each tab. Then if we bookmark a Web page, that site's favicon is stored along with the link and the bookmark's descriptive text. When we scroll through our Web bookmarks, the favicon is the first thing we see, followed by the descriptive text.

How cool is that? You get to plant your favicon brand on the machine of anyone who bookmarks your site. The only problem is that these little visuals are only sixteen pixels square. That's not

CHASE Home: Personal
ABC.com
Pinterest
Stanford Tech Commons
Seatrain Lines
Univision.com
Showtime : Home
Smithsonian
American Film Institute
Lincoln Center
New York University
O-I Home
PBS: Public Broadcasting
The New School
United Airlines
Avery Worldwide
Time Warner, Inc.
Google
AT&T Cell Phones
NCR
Ace Books – Penguin
Del Rey and Spectra
Baen Books Science Fiction

Browser News: Resources
Identifont - Amelia
New York Architecture
Tor | Forge 'oster
Book Covers
Sleevage
Smashing Magi
Amazon.com
chapters.indigo
CreateSpace
Home – Relic.com
YouTube
Treyarch
WORKBOOK
Will Terry – Blog
Writer's Digest – Books
Bibliomania
DeviantArt
English Idioms
Apple Computer
resources for word lovers
Dramatica.com
Edwardo Gonzales r

Microsoft
| KROME STUDIOS |
Barnes & Noble.com
GearboxSoftware.com
Longtail Studios
Free Images
Adobe
Scholastic
Picture Books
Random House – Books
Teenuh Foster Represents
Jim Hanson Artist Agent
Home | LinkedIn
Reto Kaul
Telenovela - Brand New
Lp Telemundo - Logopedia
PYR | science fiction
Symbols and Logos
S seeklogo.com
Logo Vector
Free Vector Logos
Saul Bass | Redesigned
Digital Painting

Favicons appear with our saved Web bookmarks and are powerful little bits of marketing, only 16 pixels square.

much to work with. And only logos free of the Seven Deadly Sins have a hope of converting directly to a favicon.

The ideal favicon would be a miniature of the company's logo, like those for Google, Microsoft, Amazon and Apple. The next best thing is an important portion of the logo, or the first initial of the company wordmark or signature, like those for Netflix, Wikipedia and Pinterest.

Unfortunately, it's hard to make a good favicon from a poor logo. Maybe the logo has parts or lines that were too fine, or lacks mass or contrast. What are a company's options then?

Making a new micro logo to use as a favicon?

Not using a favicon at all?

Or, admitting total defeat, adopting a totally new micro logo that has no resemblance to the original identity?

Who would want to do that?

See for yourself.

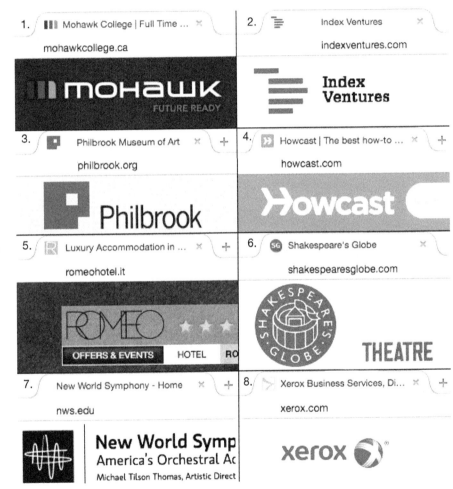

Here are the web browser tabs, URLs and identities of eight companies, right off their own websites, pixel for pixel. **1** through **3** show good, solid logos that, in turn, allow good, solid favicons. **4** & **5** use a recognizable part of their identities, a reasonable alternative to the whole logo, to make serviceable favicons. **6** had to redesign a micro logo using the same overall shape and color of the main logo, which could never be a favicon because of its lines that are too small. **7** has the same issue of lines too small but opted to forego having a favicon at all, a lost opportunity. And **8**, the Xerox logo, suffering from design flaws even at the full size shown here, is unsuitable for a favicon. Instead of not using one, or designing something to at least remind us of the logo, they use a totally unrelated graphic. Where is the logic in that?

One might suppose that the latest modern fads and fashions of logo design would be most compatible with the latest technology and media. But the opposite is true. Over an over we see that the core principles of logo design we've spoken of in this book are not only valid today, but give better results with today's newest media. What could be more modern than a favicon?

Far from being passé or old-fashioned, these principles are fundamental, even eternal. As we've stated before, trends are temporary and, in the end, will be replaced. That is the very meaning of the word trend, isn't it? So avoid trends—especially just the outward trappings of trends—at all costs.

Instead, let us seek in our corporate identity design that which aspires, at least, to permanence.

Final Words

A Shift in the Industry

I am not the proverbial voice crying in the wilderness. Many designers and companies see that much of the "new trends" in logo design just don't work—or at least they don't work in enough situations that they have redesigned their own logos to correct these flaws.

The cost of redesigning a corporate identity can be significant. But that is nothing compared to implementing the redesign throughout a company's website, stationery, signage, business forms, vehicles and so much more. For a small or mid-sized company the expenditure can be in the thousands or tens of thousands of dollars; for a large company it will surely be in the hundreds of thousands. Still, these companies have realized that their existing logos aren't working like they should. These business owners don't know about the Seven Deadly Sins of Logo Design but they still see the effects, and are willing to pay to get rid of them.

All these companies recently corrected Deadly Sin #1: Must work in black (or some other flat color).

Most of these recent identity changes fixed issues spoken of in this book. **1** & **2** Both Philips and Radio Shack simplified their logos and gave them more mass. **3** Yellow Pages took their monogram out of a containing box and made it flat. **5** Airbnb got more contrast and more readable type. **6** Domino's took its name out of the logo. **7**, **8**, **11** and **12** added logos to their identities but **12** Oxford Dictionaries gave their signature less contrast. **9** Morning Edition traded in their weaker logo for a stronger wordmark. **10** Pandora decreased its counter-productive extra letterspacing and got type with more mass. **13** Netgear also decreased its extra letterspacing and chose a color that is less likely to be mistaken for black. Of all these, only **4** Spotify made things worse: not only did they not fix their irregularly drawn arc lines, they also gave their signature less contrast by changing it to green. Eliminating any of the Seven Deadly Sins of Logo Design has always invariably made any identity stronger. Fads come and go but those principles don't change.

Learning from History

Before the Renaissance, artists knew that parallel lines in architecture appeared to taper at different angles, but their attempts to show this realistically in painting were inconsistent at best.

It wasn't until 1425, when Filippo Brunelleschi figured out the underlying principles of linear perspective. Because of that, artists could finally create paintings with realistic perspective.

Was his revolutionary idea rejected by his artistic peers? Did that discovery remain hidden in a monastery library for centuries before being generally adopted by the painting community? No. All the leading artists of the Renaissance quickly adopted the principles of linear perspective.

Because it worked.

In the mid-1800s, a chemist named Eugene Chevreul became the dyemaster for the Gobelins Tapestry Works and experimented with the visual effects

Pietro Lorenzetti, Birth of the Virgin, 1342. All the lines that should be parallel don't converge at one vanishing point as we know they should according to the principles of linear perspective.

The Delivery of the Keys (detail)v, 1481–1482. Pietro Perugino was among the first artists to adopt Brunelleschi's principles of linear perspective, which allowed artist to not only draw architecture accurately but correctly calculate the sizes of bodies in a three dimensional space.

Olive Trees (detail), 1854. Vincent Van Gogh and other impressionists and post-impressionists reveled in what they could do with color using Chevreul's principles of simultaneous contrast.

of combining threads of different colors. He formulated the theory of simultaneous contrast of colors after observing that threads of very different hue look richer when next to each other. Many of the impressionists and post-impressionists were thrilled with the practical application of Chevreul's principles. Vincent van Gogh even kept balls of different colored yarn to work out specific color combinations. His paintings, more than those of other painters of his time, resembled separate threads of color. And what beauty van Gogh created with the principles Chevreul discovered!

It doesn't matter where knowledge comes from; when we find true principles, we would do well to adopt them.

To those who see the validity of what I've presented in this book, I say, it's not enough to accept it. Any art form requires practice and discipline. But practice and discipline, over time, brings mastery. There is no need to grope one's way blindly. Even so, the labor of branding design is labor indeed.

But when your branding design works, you may have created something that will touch thousands of lives and be useful for decades, perhaps even forever.

Appendix 1: Glossary

Bitmap - a pixel based image, such as a photograph or image created in Photoshop, as opposed to vector based imagery.

CA Phrase - (see Corporate Activity Phrase)

Contrast - A difference in value between visual elements that determines legibility.

Contrast Differential - The percent of the difference in value between an element and its background.

Contrast, Excellent - 60% difference between the value of type and its background

Contrast, Minimum - 40% difference between the value of type and its background

Core Principles - Principles which do not change with fad or fashion, fundamental truths of identity design.

Corporate Activity Phrase - A word or words that concisely describes what a company does. This CA Phrase is added to a corporate identity for use in all out-of-context situations like signage, vehicles and also sometimes on business cards and advertising.

Creativity - The ability to solve problems

Favicons - Small 16 pixel square identifiers that are seen in some internet browsers in the address bar or in a list of saved bookmarks.

Flourishes - A decorative addition to typography that should not interfere with a word's core letterforms.

Functional Name - The name by which a company is commonly known, usually not including such legal endings such as inc., incorporated, corporation or company, unless that is how the name is commonly used by customers.

Golden Mean, Golden Section - A proportion, roughly 1 to 1.666, discovered by Greek geometricians and which also appears frequently in nature; they considered it a divine proportion.

Halftone - Tiny dots that simulate grays when used together to break down a photographic image for printing.

Hue - The difference between colors in the rainbow or in the spectrum, as red is a different hue from orange or yellow.

Internal Contrast - The 40% minimum value difference between elements in an identity that allows for easy recognition of those elements.

Japanese Mon - A logo-like symbol that is historically used in Japanese families to identify themselves.

Kerning - The act of adjusting the horizontal spaces between letters in larger type to make the words look more visually cohesive, called tracking in most software programs.

Law of Thirds - A principle of that proposes that an image composition will be more dynamically balanced if dominant elements are placed at roughly one third/two thirds points in a picture plane.

Legibility - When visual elements can be easily seen and deciphered.

Letter-spacing - The amount of horizontal space between letters in words; also called tracking in most software programs.

Ligatures - a joining of two or more letters in a word to make the word read better. This can be accomplished by overlapping letters or by actually rendering them as joined.

Linear Perspective - A principle discovered by Filippo Brunelleschi that parallel lines rendered to simulate three dimensional reality will converge at a single vanishing point.

Logo - A unique symbol for representing the identity of a company; sometimes also called a brand.

Monitor Gamma - The native brightness setting for monitors. For PCs it is set at 0.45; for Macintosh at 0.55 (brighter).

Monogram - A kind of logo that shows the first initial or initials of the company's name.

Pixel Mush - When the elements of an image are so fine that there is not even one whole pixel that can show either the object color or the background color but rather some intermediate color.

Prima-Donna - a temperamental person who believes that adulation and deference are his/her due and who does not accept criticism or direction.

Professional - A person who performs duties with competence always in the client's best interest.

Reversing - The placing of lighter objects, especially type, over a darker background.

Saturation - The richness or dullness of a color.

Sculpted Type - Words on a curved, non-linear baseline

Self-Brainstorming - a technique for generating concepts with oneself by concentrating on different conceptual approaches and documenting every idea without evaluating them.

Shallow Containment - The act of surrounding a signature with a shape, which adds very little design value added.

Signature - The functional name of a company written in a particular font.

Surprinting - The placing of darker objects, especially type, over a lighter background.

Swashes - A curvilinear decorative addition to typography that should not interfere with a word's core letterforms.

Tints - A flat shade in printing produced by a uniform grid of halftone dots, described as percentages of the ink color with 100% being solid ink, 0% being no ink and the grays in between in accurate percentages of how much paper is covered by the halftone dots.

Tracking - In most software programs the adjustment of the horizontal space between letters in words; also known as letterspacing.

Type Warp - A tool in various graphic computer programs for producing sculpted type. Not recommended due to its inability to treat letters individually but whole words.

Value - The lightness or darkness inherent in any color.

Vanishing - The condition brought about by objects or type and their background being close in both value and hue.

Vector - a kind of graphic computer program that produces infinitely scalable output, as opposed to bitmap or pixel based imagery.

Vibrating - The condition brought about by objects or type and their background being close in both value but very different in hue.

Visual Logic - The way visual elements create expectations in the viewer's mind.

Wannabe - A person who wants to claim achievement without learning the discipline necessary to achieve it.

Wordmark - The company name created with some unique graphic element besides just the font used.

Appendix 2: Logos by A. Michael Shumate

Sparrow Communication
(Advertising Agency)

Confederation
Conference Centre

David Luke Associates
Management Consultants

Expertise Exchange
St. Lawrence College

Eastern P. E. I.
Chamber of Commerce

Xpansion Software
(Online Vendor)

Tech Value Net
Heyland Medical

CareNet
Heyland Medical

Critical Care Nutrition
Heyland Medical

Zap the Vap
Heyland Medical

Clinical Eval Research
Heyland Medical

Latimer Soapworks

Small Business Assistance
DREE Canada

Tourism Destinations
DREE Canada

Professional Development
DREE Canada

Kingston Arts Council

DesignEd Books
Imprint of Boheme Press

Corp-ID-Man

Millennial Goals
Kingston District of the C.J.C.L.D.S.

NetWorld Magazine
Online Teacher Resources

Nature Illustration

Artisans on Main

Explore Economics East
Business Conference

Kane Associates
Management Consultants

Elementary Science & Technology
Queens University

Elfstone Press

Lamb and Lion

Visual Entity

Index

Also by
A. Michael Shumate

**Writers, Musicians, Filmmakers,
Visual Artists, Dancers, Actors**

Learn to answer these essential questions:

- What factors contribute most to success in the arts?
- Do you have enough talent?
- What do you need besides talent?
- What are the myths about creativity?
- What is real creativity and how do you cultivate it?
- How do you get through tough times?
- How do you deal with criticism?
- How do you "get the breaks" in your field?
- What foundation principles don't change?
- How do you hang on to the important things in life?
- How do you keep from "selling your soul?"
- What if you don't make it?
- Save years of trial and error
- Avoid the common pitfalls of creative careers
- A mentor in a book

Available in print and for Kindle from Amazon.com

THE **PRO KNOW-HOW** BOOK OF
SUCCESS IN THE ARTS
What It Takes To Make It In Creative Fields

A. Michael Shumate

Partial Table of Contents

Section 1: Personal Experience
To Catch A Monkey
Eat an Elephant
Challenging Decisions

Section 2: Talent
Everybody has some talents
The Magic of Talent
Inclination, Aptitude and Skill
Talent and Tangent Skills
Craft
Discover Your Talents
Definition of talent
Personal Strengths
Nurture or Nature?
Models of Talent
Why Worry About It?
What Creativity Isn't
What Creativity Is
Thinking Outside the Box
Using Your Back Burner

Section 3: Smarts
Using Your Smarts
Learning Tricks
Seek a Mentor
Cultivate Challenging Peers
Conventions, Rules and Principles
Popular Art or Purist?
Getting the Breaks
Luck or Leverage?
Get Out There
Underestimating Your Profession
Work Your Plan
The Art of Sacrifice
Marketing Yourself
Attitude Equals Altitude
Networking
Don't Pop Your Own Bubble
Influence, Homage and Plagiarism
Finding Your Own Voice
Never Stop Learning
Prima Donna or Professional
The Balancing Act

Section 4: Heart
Paying Your Dues
Einstein, Mozart and da Vinci
Stretching Yourself
Tough Times
Face Your Bullies
Facing Criticism
Personal Taste
Valid Criticism
Consider Your Sources
You Still Have to Be Yourself
Getting and Giving
Life As Art
Teaching to Give Back and Learn
No One Wants to be a Wannabe
Don't give up
What If I Don't Make It?
The Journey and the Destination

CPSIA information can be obtained
at www.ICGtesting.com
Printed in the USA
LVOW05s0012140517

534456LV00007B/41/P